# Letters From My Dead Sister

## Naomi Lane

©October 15, 2022 in Canadian national archive

# Contents

| | |
|---|---|
| Disclaimer | vii |

## Part One
## Life Before Ottawa

| | |
|---|---|
| Childhood | 3 |
| Sibling Bonds | 10 |
| Xmas Presents | 14 |
| Trip to England | 17 |
| Birth Order | 20 |
| Teenage Appearance | 23 |
| Sensitive and Caring | 26 |
| Periods | 28 |
| Smoking Cigarettes | 31 |
| Jenna Stories 1 | 33 |
| The Talk | 35 |
| Stray Cats | 37 |
| The Entourage | 39 |
| Pool Table | 44 |
| The Beach | 48 |
| Good Advice | 53 |
| Gonorrhea | 55 |
| Caribou Pub | 60 |
| Driving in Cars | 64 |
| Susan | 67 |
| Lydia Stories | 69 |
| Lovers and Friends | 72 |
| Smith Ave. House | 78 |
| Funny and Smart | 81 |

## Part Two
## The Letters

| | |
|---|---|
| Introduction Part 2 | 87 |
| Alberta: August 1977 | 90 |
| Notes: August 1977 | 92 |
| Summer 1982 | 94 |

| | |
|---|---|
| Notes: Summer 1982 | 95 |
| July 1982 | 96 |
| Notes: July 1982 | 99 |
| July 1983 | 101 |
| July 1983: Notes | 104 |
| August 1983 | 106 |
| Notes: August 1983 Ottawa | 110 |
| Late August 1983 | 112 |
| Notes: Late August 1983 | 115 |
| September 1983 | 117 |
| September 1983 | 118 |
| Notes: September 1983 | 121 |
| Fall 1983 | 123 |
| Notes: Ottawa Fall 1983 | 127 |
| December 1983 | 129 |
| Spring 1984 | 130 |
| Spring 1984: Notes | 133 |
| Summer 1984 | 135 |
| Notes: Summer 84 | 138 |
| Summer 1984 | 140 |
| September 1984 | 145 |
| Overview: The Birth of Her First Child | 146 |
| October 1985 | 148 |
| Notes: October 1985 | 151 |
| October 1985 | 152 |
| Notes: October 1985 | 155 |
| October 1985 | 157 |
| Notes: October 1985 | 161 |
| Late October 1985 | 164 |
| Notes: Late October 1985 | 167 |
| November 1985 | 169 |
| Notes: November 1985 | 172 |
| Telephone conversation from Montreal | 174 |
| Late 1985 | 177 |
| Notes: Late 1985 | 179 |
| February 1986 | 181 |
| February 1986 | 183 |
| Notes: February 1986 | 186 |
| June 1986 | 188 |
| Notes : June 1986 | 190 |
| July 1986 | 192 |
| Notes : July 1986 | 194 |

| | |
|---|---|
| July 1986 | 196 |
| Notes: July 1986 | 199 |
| August 1986 | 201 |
| Notes: August 1986 | 203 |
| October 1986 | 205 |
| Notes: October 1986 | 208 |
| January 1987 | 210 |
| Note: January 1987 | 212 |

## Part Three
## Motherhood and Beyond

| | |
|---|---|
| Coming Home | 215 |
| Mum Chat | 217 |
| Dad Chat | 221 |
| Whistler | 225 |
| Good Parenting | 228 |
| The Joe Years | 233 |
| Prison | 237 |
| Young Adults | 240 |
| Our Father's Passing | 243 |
| Battles | 247 |
| Beach Walks | 251 |
| Travel | 254 |
| Jenna Stories 2 | 256 |
| After Rosanne's Passing | 260 |
| Celebration of Life | 262 |
| Her Estate | 264 |
| Estrangement and Regret | 268 |
| A Better Life | 271 |
| A Bipolar Life | 273 |
| | |
| Footnotes | 281 |
| Bibliography | 285 |
| Also by Naomi Lane | 287 |

# Disclaimer

This work is based upon real events from my own memory and the memories of several other people who were there. Certain scenes, dialogue, and characters were created for the purpose of fictionalization. All the names have been changed to protect people's identities.

# Part One

## *Life Before Ottawa*

# Childhood

ACCORDING TO MY MOTHER, WHEN MY SISTER ROSANNE WAS BORN, SHE was menstruating. I said that was ridiculous, until I looked it up online and found out it's really a thing. Apparently, there's a big drop in estrogen to the baby when she detaches from the mother, and this can cause a mini period.[1] This information blew my mind because it seemed to set the stage for how my sister's hormones would tend to dominate her youth.

My Uncle famously told me, during one of my adult visits, that my sister was already so precocious at age six that he felt uncomfortable being around her. I took this to mean she was flirting with him. He was a gay man so this could never have led to anything sinister, but nonetheless, it set off alarm bells in my mind.

Don't get me wrong, we had a normal middle-class upbringing with two older university-educated European parents in suburbia outside Vancouver, Canada. There were plenty of moments of innocence. I fondly recall playing Barbies, riding bikes, go-go dancing in flowered palazzo pants to our forty-five rpm records and playing kick-the-can outside with the neighborhood kids. Rosanne was five years older than me, so every ounce of her attention was flattering to me. It was the sixties, and she was my cool big sister who knew more about everything than I did.

The European difference was that everyone walked around naked in our house, and nobody hid their bodily functions. We were all unabashedly outspoken and would belch or fart at the dinner table to great laughter. My mother and sister would change their tampons in front of me or wash their genitals with a washcloth at the sink. Nothing was left unsaid, and nobody repressed any emotions. There were loud opinions about everything and Rosanne's swearing vocabulary was especially impressive. I learned from the best. Strangely, nobody ever said, "I love you," but it was definitely understood. Perhaps Rosanne felt unloved at times, and I know she frequently felt unlovable, but our parents were as solid as they come in terms of providing a base camp.

We took family trips to Tofino every summer and we both loved swimming in the ocean for hours and gazing into the tidal pools of the wild west coast. We would later be drawn to the seaside as adults and create lives of our own along the coast. I am grateful to my parents for these character-building experiences.

Rosanne learned very young, as a pubescent, rapidly developing girl of twelve, that she could bat her eyelashes and smile at her male teachers to get what she wanted. She even talked about this openly at home. I remember Rosanne, at age eleven, explaining very matter-of-factly in the kitchen after school how she has used her feminine wiles on her male teacher to get out of staying for detention to complete an overdue project. She said she "turned on the water works" (crocodile tears) and that this worked like a charm. My mother shook her head in lamentation, but I think she was secretly amazed and perhaps a little impressed. My mother was a shy, homely woman who had never used her feminine wiles for anything, so this was out of her realm. My father would just roll his eyes. They should have been more concerned.

Rosanne started developing breasts very young, around age ten or eleven, and soon had the largest breasts in town. They were magnificent. So, by the time she left elementary school, there were already boys lined up to spend time with her and some of them were much older. My parents tried to fend them off for the first while but soon gave up. I remember driving down to a house with my dad to pull her out of a situation with a young man of about eighteen when she was thirteen. The young man gaped at us from the front door as we drove away with Rosanne loudly protesting.

She then became deeply affected by every menstrual cycle. I remember feeling very concerned when she would cry for hours, apparently over nothing. I was too young to understand hormones and I can see now that this was the start of a lifelong struggle with depression. The doctor put her on the pill to alleviate the heavy periods, which helped somewhat, but she never got diagnosed and treated for depression until years later.

She lost her virginity to Jeffrey Carson in the small house directly behind ours. She announced it proudly to me afterwards. I would imagine the scene in my own way, not fully understanding how intercourse worked. Prominent in the scene in my mind was his brown afro hair and a lot of kissing and groping. She said she loved him and that was good enough for me.

At thirteen, she announced to my parents at the Naugahyde orange nook in our kitchen, that she was going to smoke in the house and there was nothing they could do about it. And so it was. She would remain a smoker for the next forty-seven years until she died of lung cancer, as my mother had predicted by mailing her newspaper articles about the dangers of cigarettes regularly throughout her life.

She also announced that she could not eat bananas anymore because the texture reminded her of giving blow jobs. I never saw her eat a banana after that.

Rosanne had an incredibly quick wit and had a comeback for everything. My mother always said she should have been a lawyer. She would argue the nose off her own face. Throughout her life, she would never take advice from anyone, especially not from Mom or me. My dad, a German Jew, said she was exactly like his grandmother Nunu; a hot-tempered bosomy redhead with all her own opinions. The key thing I realize now is that Nunu was one of the few of his tribe who survived the Holocaust, so her wits served her well. She lived in a menage-a-trois with her husband and my "uncle" Obi (some sort of cousin) in England after the war.

Rosanne used her wits constantly to get out of all kinds of dicey situations. She was funny as hell and could turn an original phrase like nobody's business. Her letters (included in this book) are a sample of how she wrote in a free-wheeling style all her own. She was drawn to writing poetry and acting in plays at school and did poorly in most other subjects, mostly for lack of trying. She would frequently skip out to be with her friends and barely graduated.

There was a shed behind our house that belonged to the neighbouring boy and Rosanne's friends called it "the shack". This became their party spot, and they would play loud rock music, smoke pot and drink until all hours. At least my parents could see them over the fence, so they knew she was alive and safe. She started using other synthetic drugs like acid, MDA, speed, Mescaline, and also magic mushrooms. It was the early seventies, and these were all readily available. Rosanne admitted later in life that she was alive because of her phobia of needles so she would never inject anything. Thank god for this small mercy.

She first got me high on pot when I was eleven. We went down to the rec room when Mom and Dad were out for the day and smoked a joint. It felt like there were elastic bands behind my knees. I got freaked out, so she told me to watch tv, drink some orange juice, and calm down. I watched Willy Wonka and the Chocolate Factory movie. I felt scared when my parents came home that they could tell I was high, but of course they never suspected.

This began my initiation into her world. As I entered my teens, she would include me at some of her friends' parties, basically preventing me from being a total nerd. I was a straight A student who also excelled at music and played sports, so this was out of character for me, but I learned from the best. I began to really enjoy smoking cigarettes and pot and drinking beer. I even tried skipping school a couple of times, but I was too conscientious to keep that up. My sister made me a well-rounded individual who could fit in anywhere. She would even drag me to bars with her friends starting at age fifteen. My parents had no idea what I got up to. After the hell she put them through, I basically got a free pass to do whatever I pleased. I kept up my grades and activities so there was nothing to indicate that I was partying.

Our father had been traumatized by WWII and had lost his parents to the Nazis so we should have been a lot nicer to him, but he was verbally abusive to our mother every day, so we hated him with a passion. He also had OCD and would fuss and clean around us, which drove us wild. We berated him every morning as we sat and drank coffee together and she smoked her cigarettes in the kitchen. We would literally tell him to "fuck off". He would come home angry every evening and retreat to his office and ignore us. Then there were huge mood swings where he would be charming, sweet, and generous, but these did not redeem him in our eyes. We were mean adolescents.

Whether she cared to admit it or not, Rosanne and Dad were kindred spirits, so I suppose it was fair enough that our parents labeled her "the German child". They both looked Jewish, with small, round heads, intense amber coloured eyes, pursed lips, and wispy brown hair. They both loved strong coffee, dry salami, thick slabs of blue cheese on their toast, and they both enjoyed smoking; Dad used to smoke cigars in his office at the end of the hall and she with her constant cigarettes. He was an interior decorator, so she got her good eye, color sense, and taste in decor from him. They both got bored very quickly with being at home and needed to go out on the town all the time to stay sane. They were both impatient and hot-tempered, an odd mixture of childish sensitivity and sharp-tongued meanness. Neither could manage money; our mother paid all the bills and tried desperately to keep his spending in check. Dad was a teetotaler; he rarely drank a beer or a glass of wine. Rosanne always preferred smoking pot to drinking, so I was surprised after she died to see that the psychiatrist had labeled her an alcoholic. I believe this was false; she never cared much about booze. She could hold her own at a party but was never desperate to get a hold of the stuff. She could easily go for days without a drink.

What Rosanne didn't realize at the time was how much she did love our father. She would later express, in a college psychology essay in her late twenties, that her own difficulties with repeatedly attracting lousy men were due to feeling abandoned by our father as a young girl. He had gone on several business trips during her formative years and had moved out west from Toronto several months ahead of us to get a job and find a place to live. I had no idea she felt so attached to him and she sobbed uncontrollably at his bedside when he died.

Our parents really did try to treat us equally, but perhaps they did play favorites with me. I cannot judge this objectively of course. She herself said she felt abandoned as a very young girl by my father's traveling absences for work. I can partially blame her difficulties in school. Perhaps she was belittled by some teacher along the way. I don't think she was sexually abused, except for one touching incident by a friend's dad, which she was very open about, and which also happened to me. There were no significant traumas in her childhood that I was aware of. Our family was as dull and suburban as they come. So, I suppose I must largely blame the mood disorder and depression as a chemical imbalance that negatively skewed her view of herself.

Our parents always separated us along these family lines. They said that Rosanne was both physically and temperamentally like the German side of the family and therefore she would inherit all the German possessions when they died. I was more like the British (mother's) side, being calm, cool, tall, fair and long faced like her grandmother so I would retain all the British memorabilia. I like to think I am calm and rational like my mother and can usually handle whatever life throws at me.

I now see this was a strange way to define one's children and it largely formed our opinions of ourselves as opposites. It never really encouraged us to see any common ground, which probably negatively affected our relationship.

Some people believe that trauma can be carried intergenerationally, which is an interesting theory. It seems entirely possible that my father's own trauma of losing his parents to the Nazis at age seventeen could have impacted Rosanne's psychological make-up. (He and his sister got out of Germany on one of the last Kindertransport trains just before WWII and were sponsored by a family friend living in England. He was sent to boarding school at fifteen and she was taken in by a lovely foster family at age eleven. Their parents and his paternal grandparents were killed. Dad then changed his obviously Jewish last name to a more British sounding one in order to join the army when he was seventeen.)

Dad definitely had undiagnosed depression and/or anxiety and probably OCD as well. He would bluster around the house straightening every thread on the carpet tassels, fluffing the couch cushions and picking up bits of lint obsessively. It's only as an adult that I can look back and understand how damaged he must have been from losing his parents. No wonder he had a nervous breakdown after Rosanne was born. He was too scared to take the pills that were prescribed at this time, which were probably Valium, the favorite over prescribed calming drug back in 1958. Our mother said she had to keep encouraging him to actually take them.

So, Rosanne may have inherited our father's mental health disorder, even though it was certainly exacerbated by trauma. Or perhaps he had already been predisposed to it from his own grandmother Nunu. Calling her "quick-tempered" was probably just a polite way of saying that she frequently lost control of her emotions and spiraled into a dark mood, like he and Rosanne so often did. It's strange how one child can inherit genes from one side of the family so strongly.

# Sibling Bonds

When we were young, we played together very well, despite the fact that she was five years older than me. I recall she loved the big life-size dolls the most, whereas I loved Barbies. We rode bikes together around the neighborhood. She taught me card games like Crazy Eights and Gin Rummy. We beaded bracelets and chokers on a small loom and we loved coloring Doodle arts together with a huge pack of fine point felt pens. Of course, we had different friends, but sometimes they overlapped among neighbor kids and their brothers and sisters. Once there was even a mock wedding in our basement where Rosanne officiated. The older neighbor girl pretended to be the man and kissed me on the lips. It felt very strange.

We listened to 45 records on our plastic box turntable and go-go danced in brightly flowered matching palazzo pants with huge bell-bottoms, pretending to hold a microphone and singing our guts out. We watched American bandstand every Saturday morning together and grew up on the Jackson Five, The Partridge Family and all the wonderful Black soul groups like the Spinners, the Supremes, The Temptations and Gladys Knight and the Pips. Occasionally, she would listen to me play guitar songs and we'd sing together to Bobby McGee by Janis Joplin. This is one of my favorite memories of her.

As we got a bit older, around ten and fifteen, we bonded over record albums and would lie on the floor for hours listening and reading the lyrics to memorize them, singing at the top of our lungs. I doubt any teenager from the present generation could imagine what dancing teenagers in the seventies looked like. There was something so uninhibited about it; arms and legs flailing around, head shaking loosely from the neck, long hair whipping across the face, and slouching shoulders were the norm. It was generally an internal state of being where ignoring everyone around you was encouraged. You became lost in your own little world. If you have ever seen the Peanuts cartoons where there's a holiday party and all the characters are dancing, that is as close as you can get.

This is how Rosanne and I danced in the basement together. We would put a Led Zeppelin or Rolling Stones album on the turntable and just go nuts. There was nobody watching, and the curtains were drawn. It was probably the most uninhibited self-expression of my whole life. When I was nine and she was fourteen, we could do this for a very long time. I can only imagine our parents' shock and awe when they opened the rec room door to yell that dinner was ready. Our dad would have most certainly rolled his eyes at us; Mum would have just smiled. They never complained about the volume being loud, which was lucky for us. They just let us enjoy this joyous time together without interfering. Looking back, it was such a healthy outlet for both of us. We felt safe, happy, and free from all worries in those moments.

We would also sing along at the top of our lungs. We knew every word because we had spent hours lying on the carpet together, reading and memorizing all the lyrics on the dust jacket. This was a required rite of passage before the dancing could begin. We would even discuss the meaning of the words and interpret them in our own way. There was no Google to look up the artist's biography or intentions in song writing, we had to guess. Their lyrics became the innumerable catch-phrase of our youth. If Rosanne was looking spaced-out at the breakfast table, I would say, "Ground control to Major Tom," to get her attention. If our parents were pissing her off, she'd turn to me and sing, "I can't get no, I can't get no, I can't get no, satis-faction!" and we would share a moment of complicity. If the radio was on in the back seat of our parents' car, we would suddenly burst into loud song, to which our German father would mutter the word "Schrecklich" (terrible) and smile to himself.

I know that every generation has its own music, but the fervor of our fascination with each song and its lyrics was a literary influence that shaped our lives. It was more important than books, school, parental lectures, or even friendships and boyfriends. We somehow knew it would outlast any of these temporary relationships and become a part of our very soul. We loved the recording artists more than any of the significant people in our lives. It was total adoration. If they had appeared on our doorstep and asked us to follow them into a cult, we would have gone without hesitation. Music was an all-consuming lifeline and for someone like my sister, who struggled with depression, I'm sure it literally saved her more than once.

At other times, she could be mean. She would insult my appearance, such as telling me I was shaped like a frog with long legs and a round belly. She teased me relentlessly about having big ears and a big nose. She told me my breasts were small and saggy, which was very hurtful to a young teen girl. I think her physical prowess was her only way of controlling me and making me feel small. She resented the fact that I did well in school, sports and music and therefore got a lot of positive attention from my parents. I think she felt like the black sheep and wanted to assert her dominance in a family that felt unfairly critical of her. Her rebelliousness became her only way to stand out and get our parents' attention. Of course, all of this was unconsciously reactive. I don't think any child plans their behavior to act continuously one way or another. It was an intrinsic part of her character. It was nature not nurture, because we had the same exact upbringing and were complete opposites in almost every way.

The one thing that really bonded us was our sense of humor. We could always make each other laugh. She did a mean Elvis and Cher impersonation. At home, she was rude beyond belief and would belch or fart as loudly as possible just to get a reaction. She would lick her fingers and then stick them back into a shared food container just to annoy my mother. We were constantly acting out Monty Python skits because this was our favorite show. We loved anything absurd. We became The Knights of Ni, the Dead Parrot salesman, the high voiced crossdressing housewife played by Terry Jones or the instructor of silly walks. We would fall over each other laughing as we re-enacted these skits.

One of the places Rosanne was truly happy was on our family trips to Tofino every summer. We drove down the old gravel logging road every year before there was a paved highway and would stop alongside the Taylor River falls to picnic on hard boiled eggs, buttered bread and a thermos of tea. Our parents would rent a cabin every year so we could swim in the ocean, scouring the beaches for sand dollars and beautiful spiral shells. We would climb on the black rocks and marvel at the tidal pools teaming with life. We would flip over rocks to chase crabs into buckets and drag giant seaweed ropes along the sand. Mom would collect periwinkles, steam them in a pot and eat the tiny snails inside. We reluctantly tried them, made faces and declared they were gross. Even our parents seemed happy here walking for miles on the endless beaches, leaving their cares behind. This is the childhood I care to remember, the only time and place where Rosanne felt innocent and free of any social or psychological drama. She could be a young teenager there and nobody cared that she had large breasts or a beautiful face.

# Xmas Presents

When Rosanne was twelve and I was seven, we were in the living room late one night before Christmas. Our parents were already in bed. She waved her hand to beckon me over to the tree and we sat side by side cross-legged.

"Let's peek at our presents and guess what they are?" she said.

I must have already been disabused of the notion of Santa Claus.

"But then I won't be surprised on Christmas morning," I said.

"So what?" Rosanne said. "Besides, aren't you dying to know if you got that Chrissy doll with the growing pretty hair you wanted?"

"Yes!"

"Okay so you just have to squeeze the present and take a guess and if you really have no idea, you can just peel back the tape on one end like this and look inside and then put the tape back on. They will never know."

It seemed like a good idea, so I followed her lead. I squeezed the first package.

"It's some kind of clothes I think."

"Well take a look inside," Rosanne said.

I gently peeled back the first corner, being very careful not to tear the paper, and peeked inside. I was disappointed by what I saw.

"It's underwear! They got us underwear again!"

"She always orders underwear from that Marks and Spencer store in England. She thinks it's better quality but it's always boring and ugly," Rosanne groaned. She was squishing her package and peeling back the paper.

"Cool. This is that t-shirt I wanted with the psychedelic peace sign on the front. I can't believe Mum actually listened for once." She closed it back up.

We peeked into a few more and then I started desperately hunting for a box that would be the size and shape of my doll, but I couldn't find it anywhere. I was so disappointed.

"There's no Chrissy doll here!" I told her.

"Well maybe they haven't got it yet. There's still three more days left. I haven't got the leather purse I wanted either." She was trying to make me feel better, but it wasn't working.

"I don't want to do this anymore," I said grumpily. "I'm going to bed."

"Okay, okay. Don't get mad at me. I thought this would be fun."

"Well, it's not," I stormed off.

For the next three days I walked around as if a little black cloud were over my head. I couldn't believe that after I'd begged my parents a thousand times for this one gift, they had ignored all my wishes. Even my dad noticed something was wrong.

"What's wrong with Naoflea?" he asked my mum at the end of the hall.

"I don't know," said Mum. "Maybe it's because Susan couldn't come over to play today because her parents are dragging her off to some church thing."

"Oh, well maybe I can take her out somewhere today like Queen's Park. I think the petting zoo is still open."

"That would be nice. Then I can finish some wrapping and prepping for Christmas dinner."

When I heard the word wrapping, there was a glimmer of hope in the back of my mind. I cheered up and agreed to go out with my dad to the petting zoo. I loved feeding the animals and they had the best slide and climbing treehouse at Queen's Park.

When Christmas came around, my doll was there, and I was over the moon. I could push in her bellybutton to make her hair grow down to her butt or retract it back inside her head. I brushed that stupid doll's hair all day long and was in my glory.

However, I was still mad at Rosanne for ruining Christmas and vowed to never peek at the presents again.

# Trip to England

AT AGES SEVEN AND TWELVE, OUR MOTHER TOOK US TO ENGLAND FOR the summer holidays to stay with her mother for a month. Nana lived in a small bungalow in Leigh-on-Sea, Essex. Grandpa was long dead, so we had never met him. Nana cooked up a storm, making roasts and pies for "dinner" (the midday meal) to fatten us up. She was successful because Rosanne would lament for years afterwards that she lost her figure on that trip by gaining twenty pounds.

We shared a big bed in the back room, which had French doors opening onto the garden. I remember playing barbies for hours there. I had brought cases of dolls, clothes, and accessories. Rosanne was either at the tail end of this child's play or was simply obliging me. We acted out every kind of domestic situation with Ken, Barbie, Skipper, and some baby dolls. There was much situational dialogue and they drove around in our proverbial shoes.

We played catch and ring toss in the backyard, then we'd walk down to the sweet shop with some coins and buy a paper bag full of candy, stuffing our faces on the walk home. Nana taught us how to play the card game Spite or Malice. Some other little old ladies came over to play with us. There were triangular cucumber and Marmite sandwiches with the crusts cut off on three tiered plates, scones with clotted cream, and plenty of orange Treetop squash to drink.

Our English relatives came to visit. Dad's sister brought our only two first cousins over and we played outside for hours, jumping on "grasshoppers" (inflatable rubber balls with a handle that you sit and frog leap on). Then we had three boy second cousins by Dad's cousin who came. They were older, more serious, and boring. Sometimes our mother's old friends from university would visit with their children and we'd get some fun playmates for an afternoon.

We also traveled by train to visit some of these families. I recall buying boxes of Callard and Bowsers candies for a long train ride. Rosanne chose the black currant hard gums and I chose the black currant jellies and I was jealous the whole trip after discovering that hers were nicer. She refused to trade with me and gloated about this until Mum told us to "give over" and I pouted in the corner. Mum cheered me up by giving me some of her wine gums.

One of these visits was to a very rich lawyer friend (Mum had a law degree she never used). He lived in a mansion and would not allow us to eat scrambled eggs on toast with our fingers, which infuriated Rosanne. She hated him after that and called him a pompous ass behind his back. She treated him with disdain and didn't want to listen to him anymore. In fact, she went out of her way to annoy him by leaving her shoes on in the house and putting them up on his seat cushions until she got reprimanded. Mum wanted to swat her but had to remain composed in front of her posh friend.

Then we went to stay with our Uncle Paul, Mum's brother, who was a confirmed bachelor, i.e., a closeted gay man. He had a small flat at Earl's Court that was very tastefully decorated all black and chrome, except for a white grand piano in the middle of the lounge. He was an accomplished stage actor who had appeared on several BBC productions. He happened to be on tour at this time; so we got to stay in his empty flat while he was away. There was a painting done by our Nana of a rooster and a bowl of fruit, so we discovered here that Nana was a fairly good artist. He had a small nook bedroom that seemed like a hobbit house. Rosanne and I fought over who got to sleep in there. She won.

Mum was fed up with us because we refused to get out of bed early to go and see the Changing of the Guard at Buckingham Palace. We couldn't care less and just wanted to sleep, especially Rosanne, the pubescent pre-teen who already wore a C-cup bra at age twelve. She probably had her period that day and needed to sleep, but I was oblivious and just chimed in to support her. We heard about it for years afterwards.

At age seven, I was Miss Know-it-all and would literally say "I know," whenever they told me something. Mum and Rosanne laughed at me and rolled their eyes. They made a bet with me at Uncle Paul's flat that I would say it a hundred times in one day and I lost that bet. I had to pay Rosanne twenty pence, which was a big deal to me. After that, I learned my lesson and tried to curtail my superiority complex.

The trip to England solidified where we came from and who Mum was in the wider world. Dad had stayed home to work and thank goodness for that. We had a much better time and bonded more because of it. We learned that women could travel anywhere on their own and this lesson served me well later in life. I felt really close to Rosanne and leaned on her to feel safe during this trip. She was my wise older sister who seemed fearless and infallible. I never suspected that she had plenty of looming insecurities of her own.

# Birth Order

I BELIEVE THAT BIRTH ORDER SHAPES US TO THE VERY CORE OF OUR being. As a young child, I felt very much alone in dealing with my parents' marital discord. I remember, at age four or five, frequently listening to them fighting after I went to bed and literally rocking myself to sleep. Our five-year age gap meant that Rosanne was already sleeping in her own room downstairs.

I didn't start talking to her about our parents' dysfunctional marriage until several years later.

I know I developed performance anxiety early on. I burst into tears when my mother told me the teacher wanted me to skip ahead a grade at age seven. I was terribly afraid, but it turned out to be a wonderful decision because I adored my new teacher and class. My parents always placed very high expectations on me for academic performance and my mother spent a lot of time helping me with my homework. Both parents would quiz me before tests, and I recall frequently crying in anticipation of them.

Then there were the extra-curriculars of music and sports. I played classical guitar, flute and saxophone, soccer, field-hockey, and volley-ball. I was always busy. My sister did none of these things. She constantly hung out with groups of friends and got into trouble. We were always treated as night and day opposites, and I suppose we really were in many ways. I can see now that this probably had a negative effect on Rosanne's self-esteem. She could see all the positive attention I was getting, causing her to disconnect even more from our parents, who seemingly failed to check in with her to ask what was happening in her life. Neither of them was emotionally equipped to support her through puberty, when she really started needing professional help.

How could two children raised in the same household turn out so opposite? As a teacher, I heard this all the time from parents. "My children are so opposite." If they are nurtured the same way, then it must be nature. Or maybe children push back against each other to create or assert their own identities. I'm not sure. All I know is, Rosanne wanted to be accepted by our family but at the same time, she wanted to escape so badly from its confines. I think I made things worse for her by being well behaved, studious, athletic and musical. I was everything she wasn't, and my parents naturally praised all my endeavors. This probably made it harder for her to feel worthy, even though she was five years older. So, she got out of the house as much as possible and looked to men and sex for validation. Her promiscuity was otherworldly; that was just part of who she was, and everyone knew it and accepted it. In an era of slut-shaming, she was like the Mae West of suburbia, unabashedly proud of her sexuality. In a sense, she was ahead of her time.

Dad came home every night from work and verbally abused our mother, complaining about the housekeeping, the supper, swearing and muttering about how "fucking useless" she was. This was despite the fact that she worked full-time, drove us to all our extra-curricular activities, and managed all the household finances. She had a brilliant mind, graduated top of her class in everything, and had a university law degree. I remember sitting at the kitchen table at age nine begging my mother to get a divorce. We sincerely wanted him to move out. It was an ugly situation.

For me, my older sister took on an almost mythical status of coolness and freedom that seemed desirable and unattainable. The fact that my parents had to constantly bail her out of various dangerous situations as a teenager made me somewhat invisible. I could do whatever I wanted, and nobody would notice. My mother never even acknowledged when I was becoming a teenager myself. There was no sex talk, no training bras, no offer of guidance regarding periods. All this came from Rosanne. She was the key into this forbidden world of excitement. On the one hand, she was all sex, drugs and rock and roll; on the other, she was just my sister. I could ask her anything and she wouldn't flinch at explaining the real stuff of life. She knew about everything that seemed taboo. When I was eighteen, I had an affair with a much older married man who was a friend of Rosanne's and my parents said nothing. I could disappear for a whole weekend, and nobody batted an eyelash. My sister gave me this strange cloak of invisibility because our parents were basically worn out from trying to control and discipline her.

Rosanne and I had a special bond, as most siblings do, which was very much separate from our parents' reality. Because of everything that shaped our lives, we felt different than other people. How could anyone understand what our family life was like? We were loud, outspoken, and sometimes abrasive or offensive. We laughed uncontrollably at the most absurd things. Our parents often seemed like grandparents because they had children so late. They didn't understand current pop-culture references or norms; they were out of touch. Rosanne taught me how to poke fun at them and see them as fallible human beings instead of placing them on a pedestal.

Rosanne always saw clearly through the veneer of other people to the core of who they were and accepted people at face value. You couldn't get away with putting on airs with her. She would cut you down to size in a split second. She kept me grounded in terms of my strong academic achievement; she wouldn't let it go to my head. I was always just her kid sister and no better than anyone else. She always treated me as an equal and I truly appreciated this.

# Teenage Appearance

Rosanne had wispy shoulder length feathered chestnut hair that gave off auburn highlights in the sunlight. Her small, rounded face gave way to a delicate pointy chin and small upturned nose. Her nostrils were slightly porcine, but in a cute way, like Miss Piggy. She had wideset, big brown eyes that turned to amber in the light, with long lashes. She had pale skin but would also tan quite brown in the summer. Her small ears looked nice whenever she put her hair up because she had a small round head. Her most defining feature was her prominent eye teeth, so her big wide smile looked a little devilish, which perfectly matched her personality.

She was of average height, five foot six inches. She had delicate hands and nice fingernails, which were adorned with many chunky gemstone rings. When she was young, she had a terrific figure, with a small waist, narrow hips, a cute bum and huge breasts. After her teens, she started to gain weight and would battle with this the rest of her life. She always blamed our British grandmother for ruining her figure because she gained twenty pounds by eating Nana's roast dinners and home baked pies.

She mostly wore jeans and fitted scoop-necked t-shirts with capped sleeves or soft peasant blouses that hung loosely at the waist. She wore runners or suede walking shoes. Her favorite jacket was a soft brown leather blazer with a fur trimmed collar and a sash around the waist. She looked amazing in it when she wore a wide floppy brimmed felt hat and big hoop earrings. With plenty of mascara, she was the very essence of the seventies. Picture in your mind the TV character Rhoda Morgenstern from the Mary Tyler Moore show and you're getting really close.

We were children of the 70's. We loved going clothes shopping together. We would go into the funky emporium shop at the mall together and ogle the beaded earrings and leather chokers and purses, none of which we could afford. We did get a small allowance from our parents each week to buy small things like candy and pop, and our parents would get us some back-to-school clothes every year, which was a real treat. We always wanted high-waisted bell-bottom jeans or corduroys and flouncy peasant blouses. I would get some of Rosanne's hand-me-downs, which were treasured items to be sure. I always admired her cool style. She taught me how to stretch out your jeans on the clothesline, roll up your sleeves, undo your top two blouse buttons, and how to use a curling iron.

She also taught me how to put on make-up. She told me to open my eyes really wide to apply mascara and accentuate the corner and bottom lashes for full effect. She taught me that eyeliner makes your eyes pop and look bigger, and she said to stay away from eyeshadow if I wanted to look naturally pretty. She said to use light pink blush for my pale skin tone and took me to the drugstore to help me select the right shade. Then she showed me how to apply it in an upsweep motion along the cheekbone. She steered me away from lipstick, which was for old ladies, and towards clear lip gloss.

Her voice was mid-range and she had sort of an ambling way of talking that slowed down your thoughts and made you feel calmer. She was a great listener and loved having long conversations with friends over coffee and cigarettes. She gave thoughtful advice to her trusted allies on relationships, sex, fashion, make-up, finding good deals, and food. Come to think of it, she would have made a great lifestyle columnist, like Anne Landers. She valued her relationships over all else and was a devoted friend. She would show up if they ever needed help.

She was chronically messy. Her room was always littered with clothes, cigarettes, make-up, perfume, jewelry, snacks, and funky little knick-knacks. She never put anything away. Her bathroom was always overflowing with products. She had wonderful decorative taste and would warm up any space with soft pastel pillows, tasseled lampshades, or antique junk store treasures. She hung beaded curtains in open doorways and reupholstered chairs with giant floral prints. Ideally, she should have lived in a French salon from 1890. She was a true bohemian.

Her pride and joy was her record album collection. Her favorite artists were Janis Joplin, T-Rex, and David Bowie. She loved these artists' wildly original lyrics and outlandish showmanship, probably because she loved dressing up and writing poetry herself. You will see, from her letters included in this book, that she deviated pretty far from the norm in terms of creative expression.

She loved anything absurd and would often laugh so hard at this type of humor that she would be in tears. She would often say shockingly bizarre things that made little sense to outsiders, but I always knew exactly what she meant.

# Sensitive and Caring

Later that same summer, our parents rented a cabin in Pender Harbour for a week's vacation in the summer. Rosanne brought her friend Debbie along. It was a blissful place, and we collected a gorgeous basket of various shells on the beach, which Rosanne kept her whole life. I remember the songs "Spill the Wine" by Eric Burdon and "Coconut" by Harry Nilsson playing on the radio in the cabin. There was a bonfire on the beach at night and I remember roasting marshmallows with another family.

After a couple of days, a problem arose when Rosanne's friend became homesick and withdrawn. I remember Rosanne being very caring and concerned for her friend. I remember seeing the two of them sitting on a log, Rosanne's arm around her, speaking gently, trying to put Debbie's mind at ease. She ended up leaving on the ferry the next morning to be met by her parents. It struck me how kind Rosanne could be when her friend was in crisis. I had never seen such a sensitive side of her with someone outside of our family.

As she grew older, she would often go to the rescue of her friends. I recall our old next-door neighbor, Laurie, was going through a bad breakup and Rosanne went rushing over there with sweet treats to cheer her up. When Laurie couldn't stop crying, Rosanne stayed overnight with her to make sure she was okay. This was the kind of devoted friend she was.

She was also very loving towards the girls that her sons brought home and often treated them like her own daughters. She would get high with them and talk to them as friends, offering them advice on various life problems of adolescence. She would share her possessions with them, like clothing, make-up and jewelry. They probably thought she was the coolest mom ever. Rosanne was always upset when her sons broke up with these girls who she had grown very fond of.

If any of her friends showed affection towards her children, she would treat them like gold, opening up her home and inviting them for meals. She loved to cook and absolutely refused to follow a recipe. She would create new dishes by mixing ingredients and spices at her own whim, often with tasty results. If her friends needed a place to stay, they could always crash on her couch. She was generous to a fault, which men often took advantage of. Even though she was usually broke, they would often convince her that they were just a little more needy until she felt sorry for them. She was, in fact, a bleeding heart.

# Periods

I woke up one Saturday morning to find my mother in the kitchen and I could hear Rosanne sobbing uncontrollably in her basement bedroom.

I asked Mum, "What's wrong with Rosanne?"

"Oh, she's got really bad period cramps and it's a full moon. It's obviously a bad combination. Good thing it's not a school day."

I went downstairs and opened the door saying her name gently.

"Are you okay Rosanne? Mum says you're having bad period cramps."

Through the tears," No I'm not okay. Everything sucks!"

More sobbing. She was sitting on the carpet in her nighty and housecoat with a thousand balled up Kleenex strewn around her.

"I'm sorry it hurts so much. Can I get you some Tylenol or anything?"

"I already took some Midol and it's barely doing anything."

"Should we phone Doctor B. to ask for something stronger?"

"What's the point? Then I'd have to go down there and I'm not going anywhere."

"Okay, can I bring you a cup of tea at least?" We were brought up to believe that a cup of tea could cure anything.

"Coffee," she sobs.
"Cream and sugar?"
"Yah, extra sugar."
"Okay, you got it. I'll be right back."

I went upstairs to boil the kettle and make her an instant coffee. Mum asked for a report.

"She says the Midol isn't doing much. Isn't there anything else we can give her?"

"Not really. She has taken the maximum dose already. Why don't you go and fill up the hot water bottle for her?"

I went to the bathroom cupboard to get this and bring it downstairs, along with the coffee. Rosanne had calmed down a bit.

"Thanks," she said, putting the hot water bottle inside the front of her housecoat. Then she started crying again. "I want a cigarette, but I don't have any," she wails.

"I can get you some," I offered. I'll just walk around to the store and come right back.

"Ok, thanks. Take some money out of my purse right there."

I got dressed and told Mum where I was going.

I walked the two blocks to our corner store to buy some Player's Light cigarettes. The Chinese family who ran the store had known us for years. The daughter recognized Rosanne's brand and said,

"Those for your sister, right?"

"Yup, she's not feeling well today," I explain.

"You good sister," she remarks. "Here, something for you." She gives me a free sucker.

"Thanks."

When I got back, I brought her the smokes and the change. Rosanne had stopped crying and lit one up.

"Thanks, I'm feeling a little better after the coffee. Don't worry, I'll be okay."

"Well, that's good. Do you wanna come upstairs and watch cartoons with me?"

"Sure, I'll come up after I finish my smoke. Go and get some breakfast."

I went back upstairs, poured a bowl of Cornflakes, and turned on the Wacky Races cartoon. Dick Dastardly was trying to stop the other strange collection of animal and human race cars from beating him around the track using various evil means.

Rosanne lumbered upstairs and plopped down beside me on the couch. Penelope Pitstop was Rosanne's favorite character because she dressed all in pink and carried a parasol. Mum came in to assess the situation.

"How are you feeling honey? Any better?"

"Yah, I guess that coffee and cigarette really helped. Maybe those pills are starting to work now."

"That's good. You can take another one in three hours. Maybe you should just lie on the couch and rest up. Don't forget to change your pad every half hour so you don't bleed on the couch."

"Ok Mum, I won't forget."

We watched Looney Tunes and Johnny Quest and then she announced that she wanted to take a shower. She appeared to have survived this episode, which would be the first of many. The monthly hormonal depression was always severe, causing her to miss many school days. Later, when she started taking birth control pills, the pain symptoms improved, but she still always got the terribly low mood regardless. We refer to it as "that time of the month" and the whole family was always prepared to step up and be nicer to her during every cycle. It just became part of our family routine.

# Smoking Cigarettes

I REMEMBER ROSANNE TAKING ME INTO THE LITTLE FOREST BEHIND OUR neighborhood corner store to teach me how to smoke cigarettes when I was eleven. Her friend Lydia had come along, and she asked me if I wanted to try it and I said sure because I wanted to impress her. Rosanne passed me one of her Player's Lights and a book of matches.

"Here, light it yourself. You need to practice doing this, so you don't look like a total dweeb."

After several feeble attempts to light a match, she gave further instructions.

"Hold it like this. Press your index finger down on the tip of the match as you pull the match back off the strip."

"But I'll burn myself!"

"No, you won't. As soon as it lights you just lift your finger off. You'll get the hang of it. Just trust me." She gave a demonstration.

I tried it and it worked. I held the match to the cigarette and drew in some smoke. I immediately started coughing like a fool and they both laughed at me. I could feel my cheeks flush hot red. Lydia reassured me.

"Don't sweat it Nam, everyone coughs like that when they first try smoking. You'll get used to it."

"But it tastes awful. Why do you like it?"

"It's cool and it gives you a little buzz, like more energy," Rosanne said. "Try it again, but this time don't inhale so hard."

I gently took another puff and started feeling a little dizzy and nauseous.

"It's gross. I feel like puking," I said.

"Well, that's enough for today. You can try it again another time," Rosanne grabbed the cigarette from my fingers, smoking the rest of it herself, chatting with Lydia and ignoring me. I watched her intently and wondered how she could handle inhaling the whole thing without any discomfort.

"What if Mum and Dad smell it on me?"

"Just tell them you were hanging out with me and your clothes got all smoky." Rosanne said. "Come on, let's go. I have to catch the bus to go meet Jeffrey at the mall in half an hour."

"Is he a good kisser?" Lydia teased.

"No, not really," Rosanne said, "but he has a car with a nice stereo and a good job so he can pay for shit. He's taking me to see Jaws tonight. I'm gonna get a large popcorn and a Coke too."

"I would be so scared. I probably wouldn't be able to take a bath for a year after that," I said.

"Yah, well, I only take showers, so that shouldn't be a problem."

We all laughed and started walking towards the bus stop. I was grateful that Lydia gave me a piece of gum from her coat pocket, which helped with the nausea. I felt all grown up walking beside them. They were so cool.

# Jenna Stories 1

One of Rosanne's best friends was Jenna, who she met in grade seven when they were just hitting puberty hard. Jenna was also developing really young and also had very large breasts. She was also as wild as Rosanne and the two of them got into an endless sea of trouble. They were a perfect match.

They would skip school together in junior high and get some older boys from the high school, to drive them out to the nearby lake. While they got high and went skinny dipping, the boys used their oversized bras to slingshot boulders into the lake. Sometimes they would return to school soaking wet and be sent home. Nobody seemed to ever call the parents at this time. One time Jenna's mother saw them in the back of a pick-up truck and they caught hell.

They were already dropping acid at the age of fourteen, which is frightening. Once they were "peaking" sitting at the kitchen table and my mother came in and asked them what was going on. Rosanne simply blurted out, "We're high mother," to which my naive Mum said, "Oh Rosanne," and carried on with her cooking like it was nothing. I think my parents had no idea what to do with this feral woman-child.

Once Rosanne was having a bad acid trip while at school, so she was sent to the counselor's office. What was the remedy? The counselor pulled Jenna out of class to babysit her. They sat and watched the boys playing tennis outside until she "came down". What a remarkable solution.

On another occasion, the two of them were partying in "the shack" behind our house with their friends and were pretty drunk. Jenna's then boyfriend was balancing on a small metal drum to change a lightbulb and Rosanne egged Jenna on to kick the drum out from under him. Jenna refused so Rosanne called her "chicken". When Jenna kicked the barrel, the poor boy broke his ankle.

Jenna's parents tolerated her staying over and hanging out. They often partied late with her parents' friends from their hotel business. Rosanne would blurt things out in a crowded room such as "I'm horny," or "I need to get laid!" Jenna's mother would look shocked, but Jenna always said, "No mother, she means it."

When Jenna got married shortly after high-school, Rosanne was her maid of honor. As they sat at the head table listening to the speeches, Rosanne sparked up a joint unabashedly. Then she made out with one of the groomsmen in the back of a car before going into her parents' house for the reception party. After the party, she passed out in the bathtub, which was filled with ice to keep their drinks cold. She woke up a few hours later with a very cold ass.

# The Talk

When I was sixteen and she was twenty-one, Rosanne came into my bedroom carrying a small paper bag. She sat down on my bed and pulled out a box of contraceptive foam and a box of condoms.

"So, I know that you and Ian are going to start fucking soon so I got you some protection. This foam will kill the little spermies before they can get up there and lock onto one of your eggs to make a baby. You just load up the applicator and shove it high up into your vag like a tampon and then press the plunger to get it all up in there."

"Okay," I said, dumbfounded.

"He's not going to like the taste of it by the way. Also, you have to pee it out afterwards and give yourself a little wash or a good wipe or you'll feel sticky all day."

"Gross. Okay."

"These are condoms. Guys hate them but they work so he needs to use one. They hate them less if you put it on so when he's hard, you leave a space at the end for the cum to collect in and then you roll it down like a sausage casing. Then after he cums, make sure he holds onto the condom as he pulls out or it could fall off when his dick gets soft."

"O-kaaaay."

"Any questions?"

"Did Mom ask you to do this for me?"

"No, I just figured she is completely hopeless, so I took the bull by the horns."

"Ok, thanks."

"No problem."

"Oh, can I ask you about bras?"

"Sure."

"Well, I've been wearing these old ones I found in a drawer, but they are ugly, and Mom has never offered to buy me any and I'm too embarrassed to ask her."

"Ok, I can take you shopping at the mall for some. I will ask her for the money. We can go on Saturday if you want."

"Great thanks. You're right, Mom is really useless. How did they ever get pregnant twice anyhow?"

"Gross. I have no idea. Try not to think about it."

She got up and walked out of my bedroom, leaving me in shock, but pleasantly surprised that she cared enough to do this for me. It felt like a really special bonding moment.

# Stray Cats

ROSANNE WAS CONSTANTLY RESCUING STRAY CATS AND BRINGING THEM home. Mum usually ended up keeping them, but on some rare occasion when they were unsuitable for our current cat group, she would take them to the SPCA. If they were injured, Rosanne would insist that Mum take them to the vet's and pay the bill to get them treated. She had a huge bleeding heart for any suffering animal.

As young children, we each got our first kitten. They were a matching brown pair of tabby sisters named Dafty and Ginger. Dafty was fat and loud and Ginger was thin and sweet. We adored them and spent our childhood years sleeping with them on our beds every night. The two of them would cuddle up together on top of the warm television set, avoiding the rabbit ear antennas behind them.

We usually had five or six cats in the house at any given time. There was the pathetic, rat-faced Binky, who couldn't meow, hiding in the downstairs rafters all the time. She had appeared one day at "the shack" over our back fence at Barney's place. God knows what kind of trauma that poor thing had suffered before Rosanne found her.

There was a fluffy ginger with the broken leg named Charlie, who Rosanne found in the back alley on the way to school. We penned him up using a flipped dining room table. I slept beside him every night until a gigantic spider crawled up the wall right in front of my face, sending me screaming back to my room.

There was deaf white Teddy with one green and one blue eye, like David Bowie. He was part Siamese and extremely vocal. She found him as an abandoned kitten in a box behind the corner store. He was long and thin with the most lovely demeanor.

His nemesis was Popcorn, a gigantic fluffy white cat who loved to be cuddled upside down like a big baby. He was the neighbor's cat, but he liked our house better. The neighbor was an elderly man who Rosanne somehow knew was moving into a care home, so we offered to keep him at her behest. He hated all the other male cats and would persecute them mercilessly. Only Dafty and Ginger were immune because they were female. Popcorn liked to eat all kinds of strange foods, like popcorn (hence the name), mushrooms, black olives and toast.

Then came Alphonse, a long-haired caramel beauty who floated through the house without a care in the world. Rosanne took him in when a friend moved into an apartment and couldn't keep him. He was completely fearless and simply ignored all the other cats. Mum liked to address him in French as "Monsieur" and he loved to lie on top of the piano while she played.

Lou was a tuxedo with short wiry fur. Rosanne begged Mum to adopt him after he appeared at the back door in the winter looking scraggly. He was a quiet fellow who fought constantly with Alphonse. Our mother cursed the two of them whilst constantly breaking them up.

Then came Orange, who had been beaten up by a racoon and had a huge wound on his side. Rosanne rescued him from our neighbor's backyard and the surgery cost a fortune. He became Mum's most beloved companion in her later years though, so totally worth it.

There was something about these poor, abandoned creatures that touched Rosanne's heart. When she moved away up the coast, she took in dogs as well and always had a menagerie. They were her most loyal companions when she was alone during her final years of illness, especially her beloved German Shepherd Sam and her favorite cat, Gypsy Rose Lee. I'm glad she always found solace in caring for them.

# The Entourage

Rosanne was always fiercely loyal to her friends and, as a teenager, had a core group from around the neighbourhood. Besides Lydia there were three guys she always hung out with. They all had nicknames: Barney, Fast Eddy, and Mouser. They partied in Barney's shed over our back fence every weekend, where our parents could see she was safe. That must have been a relief because they knew she was drinking, smoking pot and having sex already at fourteen, so better that she should stay close to home. I watched them with envy from my bedroom window and dreamed of the day I might be so cool.

This was the seventies, when guys wore their hair shoulder-length. Their uniform was a jean jacket or a Mack jacket, black Dayton boots, or tan suede Wallabees. All the girls had feathered hair, high waist jeans with crop-shoulder t-shirts with bubble letter logos. Every shopping mall had a custom-design t-shirt store where you could choose your favorite decal and have it ironed onto a plain t-shirt of any colour. Popular logos were the Bugs Bunny characters, happy faces and cool cars or bands. The girls wore lots of eye make-up, especially pale blue eye shadow, and long dangly beaded earrings with leather braided chokers. They carried Mexican leather purses with tassels or braided straps. Girls wore Mexican huarache sandals in summer and Wallabees or Adidas runners were in vogue too (because Nike didn't exist yet).

Gradually the parties got bigger, and the friendship circle grew. There were a pair of cousins who Rosanne dated off and on for years, alternating between Will and Dane. They fit into the category of the strong, silent type. I tried to engage in conversation with them and they could barely get a few words out. I couldn't understand why this would appeal to my wordy sister; but they were good looking and cool, so I guess they didn't need to converse. Will also had a Harley Davidson motorcycle, so this was also appealing.

These two cousins had a sister named Leah, who Rosanne would really connect with in her early twenties. Leah married a guy with three brothers, who Rosanne then also got involved with. After dating one of the older ones for a while, the youngest showed up and she was smitten.

I think Rosanne always longed to be a part of someone else's big family because our parents were so boring. They were much older (everyone thought they were our grandparents) and European. They sat around reading newspapers and drinking tea and never did anything. Rosanne repeatedly dated guys who had big boisterous families who liked to party. She desperately wanted a family who understood her need for a wilder, more exciting life. She wanted a mother who could relate to her feminine wiles and talk about men, sex, fashion, anything relevant to her.

If one of these boyfriends with one of these big families had ever proposed to her, I think she would have married them just for the family life, but alas, it never was to be. I don't understand why this never happened because there were plenty of long-term suitors. Perhaps they sensed that Rosanne had some mental health issues? Perhaps she was too clever, sarcastic and outspoken and this scared them off? I really have no idea. It's tragic to think that she was used over and over as a sexual plaything without ultimately receiving the respect from any of these men to make it permanent. I don't even recall her getting a promise ring from a boyfriend.

Rosanne's bedroom was downstairs in the rec room. It was the biggest room that ran the whole length of the house. It had red shag carpeting, was cozy and dark, with a single window looking out to the carport.

Her double bed was at one end, with a metal clothes rack, a dresser, a side table and a mirror. Her clothes and shoes were strewn everywhere. There was a mountain of cosmetics and toiletries atop the dresser. Her earrings and necklaces hung from a slack piece of cord pinned across the wall. Empty cigarette packages and their silver foil liners littered the space. A dirty ashtray adorned the window ledge.

At the other end of the room was the pool table, surrounded by various band posters. Robert Plant, Jim Morrison, Roger Daltrey, and Janis Joplin watched over. Rosanne's prized stereo stood at the far end. It was a simple turntable on a stand with two small built-in speakers underneath, but to her it was everything. It represented her escape from the doldrums of everyday life.

―――

When Rosanne was sixteen and I was eleven, she came home one day, grabbed my arm, and pulled me down to the basement.

"Come here," she said urgently, under her breath.

"What? What's going on?" I asked.

"Look at this cool top and mini-skirt I got."

She pulled them out of her oversized purse. It was a lacy pink peasant blouse with tiny flowers around the neckline and a clingy brown mini skirt.

"Wow, so cool! How much were they?"

"They were free!"

"How come?" I asked innocently.

"Because I stole them," she grinned ear to ear.

"Rosanne! You're terrible! What if you got caught?"

"I'm not getting caught. That's why I have this big purse. Lydia does it all the time and she's never been caught. You just have to take two of the same item stuck together in with you, and then come out with one."

"But what if you do get caught? Won't you go to jail or get a criminal record or something?"

"Don't worry. I'll be fine. Jenna got caught once and all they did was take the stuff back and phone her parents to come and get her."

"Really? I'm surprised. I thought you could go to Juvie for doing shit like that."

"Maybe if you got caught like ten times or something, but nah, you'd have to rob a gas station with a knife or something to go to Juvie."

"Juvie" was a youth detention center in the nearby suburb of Burnaby that had reached mythic proportions in our minds. Only the worst possible kids got sent there for the worst possible offenses, like gang fights with weapons, dealing drugs or armed robbery. We had heard of a couple of baddies from our town who ended up there, but we always assumed they were from rough families who didn't raise them right.

"Well, what if Mum and Dad ask where you got the money for them?"

"I'll just say that I had some leftover birthday money from Lydia that I was saving up. Stop worrying. It will all be fine."

I was taken aback by her brazenness. I really felt that she had crossed a line and I couldn't relate to who she was in that moment. I felt my sister had somehow shifted away from me in attitude and values and I looked at her with different eyes. Suddenly, I no longer trusted her actions to be safe or smart. I had always admired her but now I really questioned her judgment for the first time. She felt foreign to me.

I would carry this forward with me as a break in our bond, even though she was right because Mum and Dad barely blinked when she showed up at the dinner table in a new outfit. I had lost respect for her and looked at her with some distrust for the first time. If she had done this, could she steal from me or from our parents? I did not like this idea one bit.

She did start stealing money from Dad's wallet shortly after this. She would only take a small amount, but it really bothered me, and I gave her shit for it. Our father was already a very generous man who worked hard. Even though we hated him for how he verbally abused our mother, I still felt protective over the sanctity of our family unit. This was a major breach of trust from within our four walls and it really bothered me. I never ratted her out though. I suppose our sisterly bond was still sacred to me at this time.

# Pool Table

When Rosanne was a teenager, we had a pool table in our basement, and she would frequently invite all her friends over to play. They would drink and smoke in our rec room with the thick bright red carpeting and band posters covering the walls. Rosanne's bedroom and stereo were down there too. It was a veritable girl-cave.

One weekend evening, she had Fast Eddy, Lydia and her boyfriend Micky, Barney, Mouser, and another girl named Charlene who they went to school with. I was sitting in the corner on the green vinyl bean-bag chair observing. This is how the conversation went:

"Hey Rosanne, you should take that lock off your window so it's easier to climb in when you want to invite Willy over," Mouser said.

"Duh, why would I do that? He can just come through the basement door. My parents are old, and they sleep through anything."

"That's good because I bet you and Willy can make some noise."

"Aww, Mouser, you're just jealous. Hey guys, how are we going to find Mouser a girlfriend? He needs to get laid?"

"Mouser, doesn't your sister have any cute friends you can screw?" asked Barney.

"Nah, she's too uptight and so are her friends," he said.

Fast Eddy weighed in, "There's a new girl in my English class from

Kelowna named Deanna who is cute. I think she might be perfect for you. She's short with sandy blond hair and freckles. She's really friendly. I could invite her over sometime to meet you."

"Sure, that would be cool." said Mouser.

Lydia pulled Charlene aside and they were whispering and giggling. Rosanne called them out.

"Hey, what's up with you two?"

Lydia spoke up, "I think Charlene likes you, Mouser. Why don't you invite her to the Supertramp concert?"

Charlene turned three shades of red and looked down at the carpet.

"Sure, come along with us. I can get you a ticket, no problem," Mouser was such a nice guy, but kind of the runt of the litter.

"Okay thanks," said Charlene. Everyone cheered.

"Yay, Mouser finally has a date!" said Rosanne. She hugged Charlene and smiled broadly.

Rosanne lit up a joint and they passed it around. "Give some to the kid," she said, gesturing to me.

"You shouldn't be getting Nammy high. She's only twelve." said Fast Eddy.

"She's okay. You should let her play the winner too, she's a good shot," Rosanne stuck up for me.

"Sure Nam, you can play the next game," Barney said.

"Great. I hope Lydia beats you so I can play her," I said.

"My sister has a little crush on Lydia," Rosanne said. I was mortified, but it was true. I worshipped the ground she walked on.

"When is this concert?" Charlene asked.

"It's next Friday at the Coliseum. We are going to take the bus down because parking is too expensive. I'm going to sneak in a flask in my sock so I can drink," said Barney.

"I'll just stick some joints in my bra. I don't need booze to be happy," Rosanne said.

It was my turn to play, but Barney had won so I had to play him. He broke and I sunk the first ball to take solids.

There was a knock on the door and Dad appeared in his underwear. They were huge ballooning cotton boxers from some other era.

"Could you please open the window in here? It smells like the whole house is going to burn down," he asked gently and smiled.

"Sure Dad. Maybe you could put some pants on when you say hello to my friends eh?" Rosanne shot back.

Dad said nothing, shut the door and left. Rosanne opened the window.

Lydia said, "Rosanne, do you want to go down to A and B Sound tomorrow with me? I want to get 'The Sweet' album. I love that song Ballroom Blitz."

"Sure, what time do you wanna catch the bus?" Rosanne asked.

"How about eleven o'clock? We could go to Stanley Park after and walk along the sea wall."

"Sounds good. I'll ask my dad for some lunch money. Then I'll make a couple of sandwiches for us and use the money to buy myself a David Bowie t-shirt at the Dog's Ear Boutique."

"Good idea. Just don't make tuna because I hate it."

"Okay salami, cheese, tomato and mustard it is," Rosanne said.

"Yum, now I've got the munchies," said Fast Eddy. "You got any snacks Rosanne?"

"Yah, hang on, I'll go find us something." She went upstairs.

"So Nammy, are you still playing guitar?" Mouser asked.

"Yah, but don't get too excited. I'm only playing classical so I'm not going to be headlining any rock band," I said.

"That's okay. It's still cool that you play. I've always wanted to learn."

I beat Barney at the pool game and there were cheers all around. Barney cracked me a beer.

"Here, you earned it kid. Nice game."

"Thanks!" I was so chuffed to be included in their party.

Rosanne reappeared with a plate of cheese, crackers and pickles. Everyone tucked in.

Lydia said to me," You should dye your hair blond, Nammy. It would look great on you."

"I'm only twelve. I'm not gonna start dying my hair. People at school would think I lost my mind."

"Yah, okay, maybe you're right. Well come and see me when you're seventeen and I'll do it for you."

"Thanks Lydia, that would be so cool," I was awestruck by this personal attention. "Okay guys, I need to go meet Willy at the bar in half an hour, so we have to head out," Rosanne announced. She had a fake ID she'd bought off some biker she knew.

"Okay sure Rosanne, we all know that getting laid comes before friendship."

"Hos before bros," she quipped. "Besides, Willy has a motorcycle. What do you guys bring to the table?"

"We are nicer than Willy and at least we have a personality," said Barney. "Willy never says shit. He's boring as hell."

"Yah, but he's a good lay, so…" Rosanne said dreamily.

"There's no hope for you Rosanne," said Lydia. "Come on guys, you can come to my place.

"There 's even leftover hamburgers from dinner if you're still hungry."

"All right! I'm going skinny-dipping in the pool later!" Micky stood up, waving his lanky limbs around, mimicking a swimmer.

"Shit, do I have to see your skinny ass in the moonlight again?" said Fast Eddy. Everybody laughed.

"I don't wanna see his red pubes and skinny dick either," said Barney.

"Then don't look man," said Micky.

"I won't," said Barney. "I'm gonna stay inside and close the curtains."

"Your loss man. It's like a hundred degrees out. You don't know what you're missing," said Micky.

They all left, and Rosanne went to catch the bus down the hill to meet Willy. I was left alone to watch TV for the rest of the night.

# The Beach

It was a gorgeous hot summer day in Vancouver. Rosanne and I were sitting at the orange Naugahyde kitchen nook drinking coffee, as usual, and she was smoking her Player's Lights. The phone rang and she went to answer.

"Hello? Oh hey, so what's the plan? Uh huh, uh huh…." She pulled the phone on its eight-foot cord over to the kitchen table to continue the conversation.

"I can bring two lawn chairs and a frisbee, six beers and my bag of pot. What time are we leaving? Can Nammy come? (She winked at me.) Ok pick us up. We'll be ready. Bye."

"Where are we going?" I was so excited.

"Kits beach."

"Wow really? That's amazing. When do we have to be ready?"

"Eleven. Wear your bathing suit under your clothes, obviously."

"Who's driving?"

"Fast Eddy is bringing the van. He has a wicked stereo in the back that we can listen to on the beach."

"Wow, thanks for inviting me. Should I pack some food for us?"

"No, they have concession stands there. Do you have any money?"

## Letters From My Dead Sister

"I have about seven dollars."

"Go and ask Dad for some money. Be as sweet as you can."

"OK, like how much?"

"Another ten should do it."

I went down the hall where Dad was banging out some Parks Board proposal on his old typewriter and gently opened the door.

"Hey Dad."

"To what do I owe this great honor?" he said sarcastically. "You want money for something don't you?"

"Maybe...Rosanne and I are going to Kits beach with her friends. We were hoping to buy lunch at the concession stand."

"How much do you need?"

"We were thinking maybe ten dollars, if that's okay?"

"Let me see what I have." he pulled out his wallet. "Ah, you're in luck. I do have a ten." He passed me the purple bill. "Well behave yourselves. "

"Thanks Dad. See you later."

"Tell your mother what you're up to."

"Ok thanks Dad. You're the best!"

"I know, especially when you need money."

---

We all piled into Fast Eddy's van, and he cranked the Doobie Brothers. There was Barney, Lydia, Rosanne, Fast Eddy, Mouser and me. Lydia mussed my hair and said "Hey kiddo. Good to see Yah."

Rosanne sparked a joint and we passed it around. I was only fourteen and felt so cool to be hanging out with them.

"Hey, pass that joint up front," said Fast Eddy from the driver's seat."

"Who is going to get tickets for the Alice Cooper concert next month?" asked Barney.

Mouser said," I can buy them after work if you guys give me the money. I think they are twenty bucks each."

"Ok, I'll get it to you on payday next Friday," said Rosanne. She was working at a bar in New Westminster.

"Then let's make that the cut-off for everyone who wants to go. By next Friday just drop an envelope that says Alice Cooper through my door slot if I'm not home."

"Hey, let's go to Mushroom Records while we're down here," said Barney. "I want to get the new Cars album."

"Cool, I've never been there," I chimed in. "I'd love to check out their selection."

"Okay kid, you can walk over there with me," Barney invited me. I was thrilled.

"You're not spending my lunch money on a record. A girl's gotta eat," said Rosanne.

"That's okay, I just want to browse."

---

After we got through downtown Vancouver, we arrived at Kitsilano. It was a huge beach and there were loads of people. We couldn't park the van close enough to play the stereo, but Lydia had brought her big transistor radio just in case. Mouser had a cooler with ice and pop and Rosanne added our six beers. Fast Eddy had brought a couple of big bags of chips for us to share. He was a big boy who liked to eat.

Rosanne and Lydia and I lay out our towels, stripped off our cut-offs and t-shirts and began to slather baby oil on each other.

"I like your bathing suit Nammy," said Lydia. This compliment made me beam ear-to-ear.

"Thanks Lydia. I like yours too."

Barney and Mouser were already chucking the frisbee around. Rosanne was checking out the scenery.

"There are a lot of hot guys out here. Look at that hunk with the long blond hair and the tattoo over there. I'd like to get me some of that!"

"Yah, he's pretty dreamy," Lydia agreed, "but I like the one with the curly brown hair by the tree. His cut-offs fit his ass real nice."

"You two are incorrigible," I said, "but for what it's worth, I like the red-haired guy sitting on the log. He's got cute freckles and nice arms."

"Yah, you're right. There's something cute about him," said Lydia. "He looks like an athlete. Maybe that's your type, Nam."

"I don't think I have a type yet. I'm only fourteen."

They laughed. Rosanne was trying to arrange herself so that she wasn't falling out of her bikini top.

"Got everything sorted there, sis?" I teased.

"Yah, pretty much. Let's go get some fries at the concession stand."

The three of us walked over and stood in line. Rosanne was getting leered at by some old pervert with his kids. She stuck her tongue out at him and pulled a face. He looked shocked and turned around quickly. We all laughed.

"What a dickhead," she said walking back while eating our fries. "He's ogling me even with his kids right there. So classy!"

We laughed.

"Well maybe you should have put your t-shirt on before we walked over there Rosanne," Lydia said.

"Fuck that," said Rosanne, "it's too hot out here. I'm not going to cover up just to make other people feel more comfortable."

We lay in the sun until it got too hot and then went in the water. Afterwards we felt all salty and stood under the beach shower-tap to rise off. Then Lydia and I applied some sunblock lotion so we wouldn't burn; Lydia was a ginger with lots of freckles and I was fair-skinned. But Rosanne went right back to the oil because she would just turn brown every summer.

Trooper's song "We're Here for a Good Time" came on the radio and we all sang at the top of our lungs. It was a wonderful moment that I would remember for the rest of my life.

Barney had to work a graveyard shift at the Alcan steel drum plant down the hill at five o'clock, so we headed back home around three. It had been a magical day for me as a teenager getting to hang out with my sister's friends and I was grateful to her for including me. Looking back now, I would use the cliché that these felt like simpler, happier times. I know we all feel this way about our young lives before the responsibilities of adulthood set in. It's a universal nostalgia, but this was a good day that still stands out in my memory.

# Good Advice

My big sister did give me plenty of good advice. The summer when I was sixteen, I got invited to a party by my best friend's brother and cousin on the same night. I had to decide which one to go out with. I asked my sister, and she chose the brother because "he looked like Nick Nolte". I am married to him today. (We did end up marrying other people first, but after our divorces, we got back together.) Rosanne always got along really well with my husband. She could read people in a split second, except for the men she chose for herself. She had an uncanny radar for any fakeness whatsoever and would call people out on their bullshit and she was a chameleon who could get along with anyone if she had to.

 Our father had this old-world idea that he would find us a suitable husband. He came from a rich Jewish family in Frankfurt made up of bankers and lawyers and he loved to be a part of downtown Vancouver civic life. Once, he famously brought Rosanne to a Board of Trade luncheon. Rosanne got all dressed up, as per his request, and sat at a round table with ten other businesspeople from downtown Vancouver. She must have been seventeen or eighteen. After enjoying a delicious meal of crab cakes, salad Niçoise, and wine, the speakers list began. She leaned over and told my dad, "This is some serious bullshit. I'm going outside for a smoke." My dad's face reportedly turned red with anger and embarrassment. She came back in after the last speaker was finishing up, just to get a ride home. They barely spoke in the car after he called her an ungrateful little bitch. She advised me never to go to a Board of Trade luncheon, so I managed to dodge that bullet.

Another time both parents took us kids to the opera, Rigoletto at the Orpheum theatre. After about fifteen minutes Rosanne leaned over to whisper in my ear, "Fuck this. Let's get the fuck out of here." Then she told our mother, "We're catching the bus home." She grabbed my arm and we left, catching two buses for over an hour to get home. Our parents were furious, but we hated that opera so much that I felt like she saved me.

She taught me how keep a "church key" on my keychain to open my beer, how to roll a cigarette or a joint, how to smoke hash using a pin or hot knives, how to stretch out my bell-bottoms jeans, how to forge Mum's signature to skip school, how to sneak into bars under-age through the back door, how to ask a bootlegger to buy booze, how to buy tickets off a scalper, how to sneak a flask into a concert, and how to unroll a condom onto a guy's penis. She convinced me to make my own doctor's appointment to get birth control without telling Mum, how to sweet talk Dad into giving us money, how to sneak out of the house at night, where to hide our contraband inside the house, how to keep our record albums from warping in the sun, how to apply coconut oil to get a good tan and how to put on make-up and curl the ends of my hair. This may not seem like good advice, but it was worth its weight in gold to me. Looking back, I probably would have been a strait-laced little nerdy bitch without her guidance. She opened my eyes to the ways of the world and brought me into her circle of coolness.

# Gonorrhea

ONE MORNING, WHEN I WAS THIRTEEN, I WOKE UP TO FIND MY MOTHER examining my sister's vagina as she lay splayed out on the bed with her legs in the air. This was quite a sight for any thirteen-year-old girl, as you can well imagine. The fact that the bedroom door was wide open gives you an idea of just how uninhibited my family was about their bodies.

"God, what the hell?" I asked, making my way blurry eyed to the bathroom.

"Rosanne has an infection from having sex with strange men," my mother announced.

"Shut up," Rosanne snapped. "He wasn't a strange man, he was my boss."

"Even worse," said Mum. "He should not be sleeping with his young female employees."

"He's not sleeping with his young female employees, Mother; he's sleeping with me!" Rosanne explained matter-of-factly.

"Well, I'll have to take you to the doctor so get dressed. I'll call and make an appointment. This is a fine mess you've got yourself into."

"Ow! Well, it hurts like fuck if that's any consolation," Rosanne said.

"Dad appeared in his oversized white cotton boxers and undershirt, rolled his eyes, and uttered one German word, "Schrecklich" (meaning terrible).

They went to see our old male Romanian doctor, who had already put Rosanne on the pill and then an IUD, so he was familiar with her sexual history. They were gone a long time. When the phone rang a few hours later, I answered. It was Mum.

"We're at the hospital now and they have admitted her. Apparently, it is such a virulent case that she needs intravenous antibiotics. She is just beyond belief sometimes."

Mum was clearly exasperated and worried.

"Oh shit, will she be okay?"

"Yes, yes, she'll be fine, but she could have damaged her insides enough to affect her ability to have children. She's a damn fool!"

"Holy shit! How long are they keeping her there?"

"Probably just one or two nights. I'm coming home now. See you soon."

"Well, tell her I will come and visit her," I added quickly.

---

I took the bus to the hospital the next day. I brought her my word-search puzzle book and some candy. When I walked in, she was awake, watching cartoons in the lounge with her IV attached to her, hanging from a pole on wheels.

"Hey Sis," she said when she saw me coming.

"Hi, how are you feeling?"

"Better, I guess. The pain is gone but the food here is crap. Did you bring me anything good?"

"Yah, I brought you a chocolate bar, some salt-and-vinegar chips, and a pop."

"God bless you," she grabbed the treats and unwrapped the chocolate.

"When can you come home?"

"Friday, they said. You didn't bring my cigarettes, did you?"

"No, I thought they wouldn't let you smoke in a hospital."

"There's a smoke pit outside at the end of this hallway. Can you go down to the machine and buy me some? I'm dying over here."

"I don't have enough money. I only have bus fare home."

"Shit. Okay well I think Lydia is coming down here later today. Can you call her and ask her to bring me some smokes?"

"Sure, no problem."

"So, like don't ever sleep with anyone with the clap eh, because this shit is serious."

"Yah, Mum said you could have a hard time getting pregnant if you ever want to have kids."

"They're pretty sure now that I'll be okay in that department, but it was touch and go at the start."

"God Rosanne, who was this guy?"

"My boss is a nice guy and men usually have no symptoms so it's not like he did this on purpose. It's not like we're in a relationship or anything. We just had a quickie in the storage room one night after closing."

"Christ Rosanne, you should be more careful. You really scared me there for a minute when Mum said you were in hospital.

"Yah, sorry kid. I will try to be more careful. The worst part is, I'm going to have to tell him now."

"Oh jeez, I didn't think of that."

"Yah, and he's married so that should blow the lid off his life pretty good," she started laughing.

"Fuck me! What if his wife blames you? She could get really mad and come after you!"

"I'd like to see her try. She's a little waif of a thing. I don't think she's ever said more than two words. She comes into the bar to do the bookkeeping and she's boring as fuck. No wonder he's screwing around on her."

"God, your life never ceases to amaze me. You really know how to pick 'em."

"Yah, I'm a real peach," she said sardonically, opening the bag of chips and offering me some.

She ended up staying in hospital for most of the week because they were quite concerned about long-term damage. Luckily this was avoided but it may have explained why she didn't get pregnant for many years, even though she was frequently having unprotected sex.

---

When I was sixteen, she took me to the doctor to get birth control pills, which I soon had to stop taking because they gave me migraine headaches. Then she encouraged me to get an IUD, which was great for about two weeks.

One night, Rosanne and Lydia took me into downtown Vancouver to see Barney Bentall and the Legendary Hearts band at the Commodore Ballroom. It was the biggest show club in town, and I was really excited. They even borrowed Mouser's sister's ID for me to use because she looked enough like me to make it plausible.

When we got in the line-up outside to go in, I suddenly started feeling woozy, even though we hadn't started drinking or smoking anything. I grabbed Rosanne's arm as everything went black.

When I came to, they each took one arm, got me into a cab, and took me to Saint Paul's Emergency room. It turned out I was having a bad reaction to the IUD and once it was removed, I was fine, but they had given me Demerol and I was high as a kite. When I was released an hour later, Rosanne was slightly annoyed.

"God Nam, could you have picked a better time to pass out on us?"

"Sorry," I said, "I have spoiled everything."

Lydia came to my rescue. "Nah, it's okay Nammy. We are just glad you're okay and it was just a minor incident and not something more serious."

"Besides," Rosanne said, "we've still got time to catch the rest of the show. I called Mum and Dad and they will pay for you to catch a cab home. Lydia and I are going back to the club."

I was too high to disagree with anything they were saying. They piled me into a cab from downtown out to the suburbs where we lived, at great expense to my parents. When I think about it, it was pretty unsafe for me to travel alone when I was so out of it but they didn't give a crap. Rosanne wasn't going to let me spoil their fun after paying for the tickets. Mum was just surprised to learn that I had an IUD, which she knew nothing about. She blamed Rosanne for leading me down this path, even though she was probably secretly grateful to have avoided the sex talk duties that she clearly had no aptitude for.

# Caribou Pub

When I was fifteen years old, Rosanne and her friends dragged me into a local bar. The legal drinking age was nineteen and this bar was notoriously strict on asking for ID. I did look older than my age but not four years older, but somehow, I got through the door, probably because it was in the afternoon and there was no doorman.

They bought a pitcher of beer and we sat in a circle around the small table among western themed decor. Bob Seger was belting out "Hollywood Nights" through the speaker system.

"So, you've hit the big time now eh kid?" Barney smirked at me.

"Yah, I guess so," I beamed back at him, feeling very proud of myself.

"She only got in because she hid behind my tits," Rosanne explained.

"Makes sense," Barney said. "You could hide a circus elephant behind those things."

Everyone laughed.

"So Nammy, is this your first time in a bar?" Lydia asked.

"Yah, of course, I'm only fifteen. What do you expect?"

"Well watch out for older men hitting on you," she warned, "there's some real old perverts hanging out here in the daytime. That old geezer slapped my ass when I walked by him to the washroom last time I was here."

"You're kidding me?" I was shocked.

"Nope. I told him to fuck off though and his friends laughed, so I doubt he'll be doing that again."

"Don't count on it," Rosanne said. "I'm sure he will do it again every time you walk by."

"She has a point," Fast Eddy said. "Once an old pervert, always an old pervert."

Everyone laughed. Fast Eddy was the philosopher of the group.

"I know that waitress from the Uptown Pub where I worked last year," Rosanne said. "She's a real bitch. She tried to swindle us out of the tip-sharing jar."

As I turned my head to take a good look at the waitress, I felt something wet and cold trickle down my chest. I gasped and recoiled, looking down the bib of my jean overalls and heard Barney laughing at me. He had just dumped his glass of beer down my shirt.

"What the hell?" I asked, wiping myself with a handful of cocktail napkins.

"Just a little initiation kid. Welcome to the club."

Rosanne chimed in. "Don't take it personally. He's an asshole. He can't help it. He comes from a long line of assholes."

"That's true," Mouser said. "I can confirm this from many years of experience."

Rosanne leaned over and whispered something to Lydia and then grabbed me by the arm and stood up.

"Us girls are going to spark a little doobie in the bathroom."

We all crammed into one stall and Rosanne pulled a thin joint she had pre-rolled out of her cigarette package and lit it up.

"Are you sure we're not going to get caught," I asked, feeling nervous.

"Nah, nobody gives a shit on a weekday. They're too busy stocking the bar for happy-hour and trying to eat something before it gets busy. There's only like one waitress and one bartender on shift right now," Rosanne said, speaking from experience.

As I inhaled, I started coughing like a rookie and they both laughed at me.

Lydia passed me a piece of gum from her purse and told me to suck on it and swallow the juice to stop coughing. The trick actually worked. We went back to the table.

Now everything the guys said seemed hilariously funny. They started playing a game pretending they were rich and planning how to throw a party with unlimited funds. They had to name all the people they wanted to invite, either real friends or celebrities. Lydia wanted to invite Robert Plant, Mouser wanted to invite Blondie, Fast Eddy wanted to invite Farah Fawcett, and Barney wanted to invite Linda Ronstadt. Then came Rosanne's turn.

"I want to invite Janis Joplin, Jimmy Hendrix, Marilyn Monroe and Elvis."

"But they're all dead," Lydia said.

"I know, but they can tell us what it's like to be dead. Wouldn't that just be so interesting?"

"I guess so," said Mouser, sounding reluctant.

"Kinda weird Rosie," said Lydia.

I decided to stand up for my sister.

"I think she's right. Aren't you even curious about what happens after you die? I would love to know, personally."

"Nah, too morbid," said Barney. "I just wanna live for today and forget about all that sad shit."

"Well, what if Jimmy Hendrix could still play guitar at the party, even if he were a ghost?" Rosanne said.

"Well yah, that would definitely be cool," Barney agreed.

Rosanne let out a huge belch and everybody laughed.

"Let's get a case of beer and go back to your place and shoot some pool," said Fast Eddy.

"Sure," said Rosanne, "but the grumps are home."

"They won't bother us," I said. "They just watch the news and drink tea anyhow, as long as we keep it down to a dull roar."

"Well, we have to eat something because they won't have enough dinner for all of us," Rosanne said. "Let's hit McDonald's on the way back."

"Sounds good," said Lydia. "I've got the munchies something fierce right now."

"Me too!" I was happy we were stopping to pig out because I was high and French Fries sounded awesome.

"Do you have any money?" Rosanne asked me, going through her wallet.

"Yah, I have five bucks that Dad gave me."

"Good because I don't think I have enough for both of us."

We all got up, left the bar, and piled into Fast Eddy's van. I felt like the coolest kid ever for getting into that bar.

# Driving in Cars

EVERYONE SAID ROSANNE AND I SOUNDED THE SAME, ESPECIALLY when we answered the phone. Friends would frequently mix us up and start divulging their secrets to the wrong person. After several minutes of enjoying this, I would say, "This isn't Rosanne," to which they'd respond, "Oh hi Nammy, can you get her please?" I sometimes inadvertently found out what she was up to this way when a friend would divulge their plans. I'd say hello and they would just start talking, "Hi, can you get a case of beer and meet us at the lake in an hour by the dock?" Sometimes I would ask if I could tag along, if it was a Saturday and I didn't have a mountain of university homework.

When she said yes, it was the ultimate joy for me to be able to hang out with her older friends. I remember the feeling of omnipotence being driven around by my cool big sister when I was twenty and she was twenty-five. She had a collector's stock dream car: a 1978 red Chevy Nova fastback. With the windows open and Tom Petty or the Cars blaring on the radio, we would sing loudly in unison, laughing at our own stupid head bopping or hair thrashing. We both felt young, wild, and free from our parents, our school, and work obligations. She would spark up a joint in the car and we would smoke it on the way to wherever. She was a queen to me at this age and I looked up to her for her independence as a working woman.

She would confront anyone verbally with her quick wit, irreverent humor and foul language. She would flip the bird to truck drivers and cuss out strangers in shops or offices who didn't treat her right. She would always chat up waitresses with that mutual respect that comes from working in the trenches and serving assholes in bars. There would be an instant recognition that they were kindreds and they would joke about the tricks of the trade.

She would always call me out on my shit too. She would scold me if I was being a "goodie-goodie" or sucking up to our parents. She'd call me a wimp if I didn't join in on something she thought was fun. She would criticize me harshly at times just to knock me down a peg and put me in my place. This is what older siblings do, which teaches the younger ones the pecking order of life. I look at it now as a healthy thing, even though it pissed me off at the time. She could be harshly personal if she was mad, like making jokes about my body or appearance and those really stung and stayed with me to this day. I looked up to her so much that she could cut me like a knife.

It's ironic how she demanded respect from total strangers, yet when it came to her relationships with men, she would put up with all kinds of shit. In fact, she became a different person altogether with her boyfriends.

She would act demure and quiet at times, trying to be cute and inoffensive. It was almost as if she knew she was a lot to handle and didn't want to fuck things up or scare them off. As the letters herein will show, she would cook dinners for these men to feed them when they got home from work, even when she had just worked a long shift herself. She would try to build a cozy home nest where they could feel loved and act as their surrogate mother. She would tolerate them blowing all their money in bars with other people and not contributing anything financially to their shared bills. She would let them use her car, do their laundry, clean up after them and generally turn a blind eye to their faults, as long as they were devoted and kept coming home and having sex with her. This powerful, independent big sister I had all but vanished in the presence of any long-term boyfriend.

# Susan

My best friend Susan, who grew up across the road from us, recalls Rosanne being harsh and insulting at times. She would make random comments to her such as:

"Are you my friend or not?"

"You'd be really pretty if you got a nose job."

As her sister, I grew to expect these kinds of cutting remarks, but they still really stung. I still don't know if this was her way of genuinely offering advice (she once told me I would look better as a blond), or if she was aware of her meanness and trying to assert her dominance over us. It was sort of a relief to hear that I was not the only one on the receiving end of these remarks. She must have appeared scathing to the outside world with her bluntness. Here are a some examples of her commentaries on my appearance:

"You have the figure of a frog with your long legs and round belly. I'm going to call you Humpty- Dumpty."

"Why are your breasts saggy if they're so small?"

"Your ears are so enormous you must pick up signals from other galaxies."

"Your nose is so big everyone can see it before you enter a room."

"Your singing voice sounds really nasal."

Coming from a sister five years older, these remarks really had a lasting effect on my self-esteem. That last one stopped me from ever pursuing singing or playing popular music with friends, which is a huge regret because I was good at chording and harmonizing. I think all these jabs were her way of taking me down a peg. She was tired of hearing me receive accolades from my parents for being successful at school, in music and sports. I was very hardworking and studious and got a lot of homework and exam coaching from our mother. This must have seemed like favoritism to Rosanne or else she was just jealous, I'm not sure. All I know is that I looked up to her for her beauty and knew I could never achieve the same level of physical attraction.

In a more positive light, my friend remembers our mother as being Rosanne's best friend in adulthood. They would sit in the kitchen drinking tea and Rosanne could tell her anything. Mum was always supportive and forgiving of her frequent mistakes. She continually bailed Rosanne out of dicey situations her whole life. It's true that Rosanne made her laugh, and I wonder if Mum sort of lived vicariously through her antics, as her own life was fairly dull. She secretly admired her fearlessness. Rosanne's storytelling was mesmerizing and almost everything she did defied belief. She lived largely outside societal norms. My best friend called her colourful, creative, corrupt and crazy. She was very lucky to have our mother as her staunchest ally.

# Lydia Stories

ROSANNE'S BEST FRIEND LYDIA RECENTLY SHARED A FEW STORIES from their teens. She remembered when they were sixteen and had a double date with two brothers. One brother had a huge red afro, the other was older and blond. They met at a graveyard, dropped acid, then went ten-pin bowling. Rosanne was reportedly the worst bowler they had ever seen. She would hurl the balls downward from chest height without any notion of them rolling to the pins. Then she and Lydia went into the washroom and became mesmerized by the colours they saw swirling in the big mirror. They ended up staying in there for what seemed like a very long time. Afterwards, I remember Rosanne dating the blond brother for a short while, sleeping with him, and telling me he was "a good lay". Lydia also stayed with the red afro brother for quite a long time. This fellow routinely wore a black top hat, which was extremely cool. I thought that together they looked like T Rex and Stevie Nicks. She wore this long brown corduroy coat with big brass buttons, which she eventually passed down to me. It was one of the greatest gifts I ever received. I treasured it and wore it everywhere. I felt so cool when I had it on because her friend had achieved goddess-like status in my mind. I thought she was so beautiful and wished I could emulate her style.

Lydia, Fast Eddy, and Rosanne used to walk to high school every day down a steep forested shortcut by a creek. Rosanne had glasses she refused to wear and was fairly uncoordinated, so when it came to the steepest part, she would sit down and slide on her ass, so she often arrived at school with a wet, muddy bottom. This must have really made the teachers wonder what she's been up to on the way to school. She wasn't inhibited by this and would walk down the hallways proudly in spite of these stains.

One day, in their late teens, Lydia and Rosanne went downtown for some shopping. Some old man leered at Rosanne's chest on Granville Street and said, "I like your noses!" Rosanne wanted, of all things, a halter top. They went into the changeroom together and Lydia plastered herself against the mirror to steady herself and said, "Okay Rosanne, take off your bra." After she put the halter top on, Lydia had to break it to her that it was never going to work. There was just too much to work with and she couldn't walk around like that.

They used to hitchhike together across the border to get American jeans, like Oshkosh brand overalls. They would wear their oldest clothes, leave them behind in the changeroom, buy a bunch of clothes and put them on in layers so they wouldn't have to pay any duty when crossing back into Canada. Once Rosanne had three bras on for the journey back. These excursions happened without our parents' knowledge of course. If the girls had disappeared, nobody would have ever known where they were.

When they got their first real jobs, they rented apartments on opposite sides of the same building. Rosanne must have moved there first because she had two female roommates, otherwise she would have lived with Lydia. There were fire escape staircases outside their bedroom windows. Late one night, as Lydia was in bed with her boyfriend, a drunken "Romeo" appeared at the window pleading for Rosanne to let him in. She opened the window and told him he had the wrong side of the building. He looked baffled. Presumably, Rosanne didn't want him buzzing the apartment so late and waking up her roommates, so she sent him to Lydia's fire escape window as a prank.

. . .

Together they dreamed of creating a greeting card business together. Lydia would do the artwork and Rosanne would come up with the caustic one-liners. This would have tapped into both their strengths. It's a shame this never materialized. I doubt the general public would have found them tasteful.

It was really upsetting for Rosanne some years later when she and Lydia had a falling out. I don't even know why it happened, but I remember Rosanne feeling insulted that her friend had asked her to buy one of her paintings instead of gifting it to her after so many years of friendship. This was the final straw. They broke off contact and never spoke again, but it really upset Rosanne. They had been through so much together and had so many shared memories. Rosanne was always extremely hurt whenever a female friend abandoned her.

I realize now, with some shame, that she must have felt the same way about me, when I would later cut off contact and become estranged from her. I really never intended to hurt her; I just couldn't deal with her lifestyle as our kids got older. I felt compelled to protect myself and my kids, but to her it must have felt like the ultimate betrayal and for this, I feel sorry.

# Lovers and Friends

Rosanne was seldom single. She had a string of boyfriends in her life who were mostly selfish, broke, and unreliable. She had a penchant for short, stocky macho men with moustaches who had a chip on their shoulder. Some of them were introduced to the family and my parents were never impressed, but they were always polite and generous with food and drink. There were also a few long-term friendships from the neighborhood who were fuck buddies. She was off and on again with Willy the biker for years and was friends with his sister and her whole family.

I never considered my sister to be a "slut" and I never heard anyone call her this in my whole life. I wonder now if girls in high school ever called her this behind her back. Some probably did, given her outlandish behavior. I never considered that she might have been teased in high school because I had always admired her exploits and saw her as simply in control of her own sexuality. She never once came home and said that other girls had made nasty remarks. I think they were probably too afraid of her lashing out verbally in retaliation. She was one of the "cool kids". She just had ferocious sexual needs that needed to be met more than other girls her age. In her teens and early twenties, she rarely took sex too seriously or got depressed about a guy not calling her back. She enjoyed playing the field and made no bones about it. To me, as her younger sister, she was a maven. She was unabashedly unapologetic about her sexuality, which was unusual at such a young age. She often said it was a miracle she didn't get pregnant during her youth and then it was equally a miracle when she did finally get pregnant at age twenty-seven, then wanting to have a baby.

After finishing high school, Rosanne took a bartending course and began working in bars. She was always a very hard worker and never complained about doing long late shifts. Her natural social affinity for talking to people made her a great fit for this type of work and she felt right at home serving a group of bikers or a party of gay men or businesswomen. She wouldn't take crap from anyone and would cleverly use humor to put them in their place if they tried to pull rank on her.

I realize now that at eighteen she began working at a shadowy strip club down by the waterfront in New Westminster. I never questioned whether she was tending bar or possibly stripping, but now I think it may have been the latter. I feel uneasy when I recall the cryptic way she used to describe her shifty boss. He sounded more like a pimp than a manager and I could tell she was ashamed of the whole situation because she was very secretive about it, which was out of character. Thank god she didn't stay there long.

There was an incident when one of the patrons, a much older truck driver, got her high on methadone. She called me in distress to pick her up in a taxi and help her. When I arrived, her pupils were big and dilated and she looked so spaced out and panicked. I stayed with her at a female friend's place and tried to keep her calm until she came down. It was the worst trip I ever saw her on.

Shortly thereafter, she abruptly left for Alberta with another truck driver, a black fellow our family had never met. She shacked up with him for about six months until the relationship went south, and she came home again. Nothing much was said about him, and this period was chalked up as a mistake.

There were two brothers and a cousin who Rosanne had relationships with during her early twenties. Their names were Ron, Rick and Jeff. They lived in our neighborhood and two of them were bikers, one of whom tried to become a local politician. Jeff was giant in stature with a very long beard, long unkempt hair, and a wild look in his unusually wide set light blue eyes. He ran a local junk store on the side of the highway. Rick and Ron both worked in the steel drum factory down the hill.

I remember one New Year's Eve; I was at the local bar with my friends and Rosanne joined us. Jeff strolled in unexpectedly, saw Rosanne, sat down at our table and pulled her onto his lap. She seemed delighted to see him. My friends looked at him wide-eyed, as though a yeti had just come in from the North Pole. He and Rosanne proceeded to get fiercely drunk together and they ignored us completely. They left together shortly after the midnight countdown, and she didn't return home for three days. She had reportedly stayed in the back of his junk store where he had rudimentary living quarters with a beer fridge, a hotplate, a tiny table, a bed, a couch and a TV. It was dirty and run-down, but they were happy getting high, drinking beer and watching game shows and baseball together.

Ron was the quiet one of the three. He was short, with black hair. He had some connections to a local organized biker gang. They had been in an on-again, off-again casual relationship since high school. They would hook up once in a while with no strings attached. Rosanne knew his family and was good friends with his sister, so she'd run into him sometimes at their parents' home. He had an apartment close by so this inevitably led to another hook-up, but they never got serious.

I think he was too boring for her because I barely ever heard him speak two words. He would say hi to me and smile when I saw him, but that was all. I don't know how she could have spent more than five minutes with him after they got out of bed.

Rick was tall and handsome with shoulder length, feathered brown hair and dark brown eyes. He was a regular at our local watering hole, so much so that I thought he was an alcoholic even in his twenties. I knew his younger female cousin from my school year, so I'd met him when I was over at her house. He was funny and would tease us merci-lessly, calling us "little brats" and "pain-in-the-asses" but then he would bootleg beer or weed for us so we thought he was wonderful.

Rosanne would have a casual shag with him now and again, mostly in the back of his car or at his uncle's place, where he was allowed to entertain women. His uncle sounded creepy to me because he would hit on Rosanne even as she was coming out of Rick's bedroom. She would cover herself up and laugh it off and make sure she was never alone with him.

As she got older, she started to have more long-term relationships and take rejection more seriously. There were several men who kept stringing her along. They lived further away, would show up in town to entertain her for a few days, then go back to their lives. Now that I consider this, any one of them could have been married. At around age twenty-five, she started longing for something more committed and permanent. I can think of three relationships where she hoped for an engagement that never came. Perhaps these men didn't see her as marriage material because they knew she was too wild or promiscuous. Perhaps they had witnessed some of her mood swings and got scared off. If she got mad, she might fly off the handle and give them an earful they wouldn't soon forget. If she felt rejected, she could easily cry uncontrollably in front of them, which may have been a turn-off if they were cold-hearted.

I think she had a difficult time asking for anything from men. She was a giver and would often be taken advantage of. She adopted the role of "little woman" by cooking and cleaning up after them or worse, lending them money or her car. I think they lacked respect for her and didn't see her as an equal partner. Our father used to say she was "scraping the bottom of the barrel" with her choice in men. None of them were educated or well-off. She was attracted to losers and low-lifes who liked to abuse substances as much as she did. She saw successful men as "stuck-up", fake, and undesirable. She would only choose partners who were on par with her depressive self-image, believing that anyone with a steady job or life goals would look down on her. She never saw herself as leaving the bubble of our little suburban life, she was stuck.

At twenty-five, she took a job at a popular biker bar out in the suburb of Maple Ridge near where her best friend Lydia was living.

She told me afterwards that she had been high on "bennies" (little purple uppers) every day for the year she worked there. I remember one incident when she drove her yellow Honda Civic drunk into the front of the motel where her current love interest was staying. Miraculously, she never had to pay damages. I suppose the car insurance must have covered it. She also told me she had a threesome with her best friend and her junkie husband at this time, which she reported as a big mistake. I was at university then, but we were still close and hung out quite a bit.

    She hooked up with a long-shoreman named John who grew up in our town and had a big family. Rosanne loved his family and felt like she fit right in. His mother and siblings loved her and she came home one day and told me that she wanted to have ten kids with him, preferably all boys. I think this loud, boisterous, partying family was the exact opposite of our own, where she often felt stifled and misunderstood. This relationship lasted about a year, and it ended with him cheating on her with a waitress from the local pub. She was heartbroken.

    Rosanne would repeatedly rescue these losers, who would sleep on her couch, eat her food, drive her car, sleep with her whenever they felt like it and contribute nothing in return. I wonder if she was even sexually satisfied in these relationships. I don't think she knew how to ask for what she wanted either in or out of the sack. It boggles the mind how such a feisty, outspoken, socially astute woman could repeatedly settle for such terrible men. Was it simply due to low self-esteem? And if so, why did she view herself in such a dark light?

    Rosanne then found a much better job working as a dishwasher at a local hospital. She began a happier period, moving in with a lesbian couple she met at this job. They rented a lovely old apartment with high ceilings. Rosanne painted the walls mauve, put big cushions all around, and lamps with tassel shades, it was the perfect hippy home. Coincidentally, her two roommates were my former volleyball coaches from high school, so I knew them too. They were highly intelligent and responsible and had a good influence on my sister. They also had a pet tarantula. We hung out together there on weekends, listening to records, smoking weed, and having a lovely time.

When she was twenty-five, she met a gorgeous eighteen-year-old named Mack, who was the younger brother of a friend. They had a torrid summer love affair that left her heartbroken. At one point she even tried to fob him off on me to avoid the inevitable heartache, but then she realized she wanted him all to herself. She knew he would eventually leave and go back east to his family home, but she couldn't break it off. That was the one time I really saw her so lovestruck that she didn't know how to get on with her life. She cried and cried over that boy.

One of Rosanne's long-time loves was Bob. He was a Viking of a man, with wavy dark-blond hair and a big beard. He drove a light-blue relic of a Dodge truck and worked sporadically as a mechanic. He lived in a trailer out in the valley and drove quite far to see her, so he seemed committed. The had a lot of laughs together and it seemed so promising that she moved in with him and their relationship lasted for over a year.

Our whole family loved Bob. He was easy to talk to and you instantly felt like he was your big brother who would protect you from the world. Even Dad loved him because of his Scandinavian roots and willingness to chat about old trains. He was the first boyfriend she ever brought home who made a connection with our father. He seemed to treat Rosanne with care, which was a nice change. He was heartbroken when she left him behind.

# Smith Ave. House

ROSANNE MET BRENDA IN HIGH SCHOOL, AND THEY SEEMED TO BE kindred spirits. Together, they moved into a small old white stucco rental house, which was only a ten-minute drive from our parents. They got a skookum deal because Brenda's family knew the owner. Brenda was very quiet but tough and could handle anything Rosanne threw at her. She wasn't about to put up with any bullshit. Brenda was an old soul who was content to love her big husky dog and stay out of any social drama. She was a true-blue friend and Rosanne was lucky to have her because she brought a grounding energy into their home, which Rosanne so desperately needed.

Rosanne had taken her decorator's eye to this space as well. There were lots of soft colors, big cushions, funky art treasures and thrift store knick-knacks tastefully placed inside. Brenda had a great stereo system, and I often went over there to get away from my parents and blast some great music. They both loved to get high, and I had an open invitation to join them, which was lovely for any nineteen-year-old university student who had done too much studying and needed a break. They even gave me a spare key to come and go as I pleased. I would house sit for them whenever they took a little road trip together and I loved walking Chaka the dog and having the freedom to invite friends for an overnight hangout. This freedom and responsibility made me feel all grown up.

Brenda was in a relationship with a British fellow called Tom, who lived in the rental house next door, which was owned by the same landlord. He was a bit of a miserable sod and I wanted to slug him in the head every time he made a snide remark about her curvy figure, but they seemed to love each other just the same. However, Brenda was smart and independent enough to know she should keep her own place and not move in with him too quickly. Rosanne was a champion at putting Tom in his place whenever he made stupid wisecracks thinly disguised as jokes. She would stick up for her friend and shut him down immediately. She was way too quick-witted and mouthy to put up with him. Sometimes she would just get fed up and tell him to "shut the fuck up".

Rosanne was enjoying one of the happiest times in her life. She was working full time as a hospital dishwasher, a unionized job, so she was making good money and she was finally fully independent of our parents. She was single, had a cool red Chevy Nova fast-back, and could date and bring home whomever she pleased, which she frequently did. She could afford to buy herself stylish clothes and go out on the town drinking in bars with her friends. Life was good.

She even loved the domestic side of life. She enjoyed cooking for us and potting plants and flowers to beautify their surroundings. She started weaving, purchasing a small loom and hanging her pieces on the walls. She liked hunting for pretty floral fabric and sewing shams for her couch pillows. She painted her bedroom walls pink to make it feel like a French boudoir, complete with perfume bottles strewn everywhere. If she had lived in another era, she could have easily been a brothel or saloon "Madam". She would have kept the unruly gentlemen in their place with her sharp tongue. I could see her shoving wads of cash into her bra while showing them to their rooms. She would have treated all the young prostitutes with care and kindness and taken them under her wing. In fact, she would have been overly generous and squandered all the profits on fancy clothes and entertainment because she was never very good with money.

For me, this period was one of fond memories between us, when we could just hang out, smoke a joint, drink a beer and talk for hours about life. Brenda and I were extremely compatible, and I enjoyed every moment over there visiting. The three of us took a little trip to Tofino and had a lovely time scouring the little shops, eating take-out, and walking on the beach for hours. We felt all grown up having driven ourselves there for the first time without our parents. We checked in at the old Dolphin Motel, headed down to the beach, smoked a joint, drank a mickey of Southern Comfort and laughed ourselves silly. It felt good to be three women, away from any boy drama, which seemed to follow Rosanne everywhere. She was much happier and more emotionally stable away from men and these were happy times, feeling connected to the wild landscape and the great wide world. I wish she could have stayed with Brenda forever because this was her longest sustained period of good mental health.

# Funny and Smart

ROSANNE HAD AN EXTREMELY QUICK WIT AND WAS GENUINELY FUNNY. She loved to draw silly doodles in the margins or make up ridiculous little poems to make me laugh. She would break into song, doing hilarious impersonations of Elvis, Cher and Tom Jones in the most schmaltzy booming voice she could muster. She would mock our parents or the neighbors with her schtick, pretending to be the overly chatty vacuum sales lady across the road or the drunken alcoholic dad of our close friends. Nobody came out unscathed. She should have been a stand-up comedian like Joan Rivers. Of course, being on the receiving end of her barbs was not as much fun because she could really sting you.

It never occurred to me to make fun of our parents, but she did it all the time.

"Look, there's Mum out in the garden. When she bends over, I get a glimpse into what our future looks like, god help us."

"Dad's in the living room hunting for buried treasure between the couch cushions."

"We should call Betty (the neighbor) to come over and give Dad her vacuum cleaner demonstration. They would be perfect for each other. Then Mum would be free to go drink with those men in the driveway across the road."

Our father would arrive home every day to announce what bargain lunch he had found in his travels around town.

"I had a bowl of soup, a ham sandwich and a nice cup of coffee for $2.69." We would roll on the floor in hysterics every time because it was so predictable and he'd ask, "What's wrong with you two? You're behaving like idiots."

I recall once she had lost about twenty pounds and when I asked her how she'd managed this, she replied:

"If you want to lose weight, you have to stop eating."

I thought this was nothing short of brilliant. Of course, she was also swimming every day at the local indoor pool, which didn't hurt either.

She had numerous pet names for me, which you will see in her letters. She called me by several Jewish boy's names, such as Arnold, Edwin, (or Edwina), or Lenny. She played with my name and called me Nairobi, Nimrod, Nanaimo. She would address the envelopes on her letters with a different name each time she wrote so I would laugh as soon as I retrieved it from the letterbox. She would attach various titles to my name, such as Esquire, Duchess of Kent, Lady or Madame. She even used to call me "Pindick the Bird-Raper." I have no idea where that one came from.

She would leave me funny little notes around the house.

"I've gone out. I'll see you when I get back. Don't eat all the radishes while I'm gone, or you'll smell worse than a camel's ass."

"The next time you see me, I'll be older, so you may need to address me more formally. Bear that in mind."

"I have gone out. There's coffee in the pot. Remember who your parents are and try not to be like them."

"I took a dump this morning that reminded me of you. Love, Rosanne."

She would walk up the stairs from her basement bedroom stark naked on her way to the bathroom, receiving the biggest exaggerated eyeroll from Dad. She would change her tampons right in front of me and tell me all about her afflictions. I learned all about STDs from her, from yeast infections to gonorrhea. She would recount her doctor's visits with our old male doctor to great effect.

"I think Dr. B has a crush on me. When he sticks that icy cold speculum up my twat, he always says something cute like, "My dear, you have been sexually active with the wrong man again, haven't you? You need to be more careful and choose wisely. Try to find a nice doctor to settle down with."

Once, when I was about nine years old, I bought her a poster for her birthday and when she opened it in the kitchen, she and Mum broke out laughing. I didn't understand my mistake. It was a picture of a drunken Sylvester the Cat sprawled out in a glass of champagne with the caption, "Everyone loves a tight pussy." I was too young to get the joke. Needless to say, I had to return the gift.

Her clever comebacks were always surprising, and Mum always said she should have been a courtroom lawyer because she could think so fast on her feet. This, combined with her rebellious spirit, is why she was so disarming in social situations. She refused to follow prevailing etiquette and would deliberately upset the apple cart wherever she went. She had no qualms about going into a friend's refrigerator and helping herself to food or drink without asking. She would sit down at a friend's family dinner table uninvited and join in the conversation as if she owned the place. She would speak to people of power as if they were equal to her in stature; no one got preferential treatment. Strangers either loved this approach or hated it, depending on how stuck-up they were. She could be viewed as a breath of fresh air or a tornado.

Life was never dull with Rosanne around. She taught me not to fear the grown-ups and to simply recognize the humanity in everyone. To her, everyone came with foibles and weaknesses. I couldn't have asked for a more entertaining sister and for this I will always be grateful.

# Part Two

## *The Letters*

# Introduction Part 2

THE LETTERS FROM ROSANNE TO ME IN THIS SECTION ARE COPIED verbatim, with out editing any spelling or punctuation. You get the raw, unadulterated language of her speech, full of silly, made-up words, and turns-of-phrase. She has numerous pet names for me and everyone else. She swears a lot and adds poetic flourishes. This is what made these letters so entertaining for me to receive.

The letters mostly come from the period when she decided to make a big move out to Ottawa for a change of scenery. She was twenty-five years old. Her good friend Wanda was out there encouraging Rosanne to come and stay with her until she found a job and her own place. She quickly met a rich man in his fifties who was her sugar daddy for the first few months. He was some bigwig events planner who helped her get a job catering some of his events. She quickly grew bored of him and moved on to become a bartender at a busy hotel bar in the heart of downtown. She reported back to me that many of the government office workers were gay men who made up a large part of her clientele. She related many hilarious stories about "her queers", who she grew very fond of. She would even go out to clubs with them occasionally.

For my sister, there seemed to be a fine line between survival and prostitution. She often treated her sexuality as a means to an end. Case in point, her sugar daddy when she first moved to Ottawa. She spoke of this man, Dominic, in one of her letters. She met him when she applied for work at one of his bars or restaurants. He was in his fifties or sixties and was widely connected around town in the hospitality industry.

Rosanne saw an opportunity. He offered to pay for her accommodation and find her a job in his catering business as long as she slept with him. He also wined and dined her and took her to summer events he was managing. Where some young women might have wanted a May-December romance, Rosanne never had any illusions of falling in love with the guy. She was far too savvy for this and knew exactly what she was getting herself into. She already fully understood the way the world worked and could be incredibly charming when she needed something. She could play the game with the most experienced players.

This went on for a few months until she felt grounded in the new city and had enough of sleeping with the "old man". She managed to extricate herself from the arrangement without offense on either side. In fact, I think from her letter, that he even found her a better job in a restaurant/ bar before moving on to his next conquest.

This may have been the only wealthy man she ever dated, having a real knack, instead, for choosing the unemployed. It's a shame she didn't parlay her tremendous social skills into finding a rich husband, since she struggled financially for the rest of her life. Even if she didn't marry for love, she could have ended up with a nice divorce settlement if she had really put her mind to it. But alas, her standards were low. She would constantly revert back to her "type", which was the short, muscular, mustachioed macho man with a massive chip on his shoulder. This was the man who refused to take responsibility for anything that happened to him. He was simply misunderstood and hard-done-by. The world had dealt him shitty cards, and everyone should feel sorry for him.

Then she met Don. He was a short, well-built Metis man with a moustache, her perfect type. He was a welder by trade and was gainfully employed when she met him. He had a large family near Ottawa who owned a small cottage on the river near Cornwall on the US border. All reports home indicated that she was in a serious relationship, and she was madly in love. Soon, Rosanne became pregnant, and she was thrilled. She had seriously wondered for years if she could even conceive because she had been having sex without protection for years without incident. Now there was talk of marriage.

I visited her once during this period, on my way to a university sponsored trip to Haiti. It was the summer of 1984. Ottawa was relentlessly hot and humid, and Rosanne was eight months pregnant. I took a room at the YWCA close to her apartment with Don. Thank god I didn't stay with them.

This whole scenario informs her letters which follow.

# Alberta: August 1977
## (Rosanne is nineteen)

Dear Nam,

You've written an even more mother letter than mother. Lecture! Lecture! I hardly drink at all now. No time. I've been working a real lot. I guess I told ma that I'm now putting the $300 to use, so put your dear little mind at rest. Give up on the Wilsons, they're hopelessly "normal". Quincy is the latest tv show eh? I prefer Quigley myself. You'll never guess who called today? Dougie the Doormat (her casual boyfriend). He's coming up here 1st of Sept. to the 12th and then coming back in another week for good. He says we'll get a place together or something. That guy never quits; must be love. Ha. It's good though 'cause it's easier to get along with one guy than two girls. I guess I really do care for him anyhow even if he is a doormat.

How old is Graham now? What will you take at school this year? I'm at work right now doing a 5-1 am shift and it's really slow. The pub next door in this hotel is a gay bar. Lotsa fun, no I never see them much but I'm not going to tell Doug til he finds out for himself. Brenda's still with us so there's 3 of us in a one bedroom. Where we'll put Douglas, I have no idea. We've been hunting for a bigger place but all the students and holiday folk are coming back to town and snaffling everything up.

*Letters From My Dead Sister*

I hope you're taking good care of the stereo and albums kid. We just had a quick-change artist in here trying to screw one out of money but I was too quick for him needless to say. In a week or two I'll be senior bartender as the other girl is leaving us. More cash per hour I guess. I'm getting in shape by walking a lot. How's the flab with you? I can eat all I want for nothing here in the dining room so I'm not spending a lot on food either. Tips pay for cigarettes and bus fares so I'm going to try to buy a car in the spring. I wouldn't want to drive in the winter here anyways.

I'm going to invest in a floor loom and perhaps a spinner to occupy myself at home. There's one going for $145 up the street which is a really good price considering the ones at school were worth $1000 a piece or something like that.

I still miss everyone when I have time to think about it but I hear all my boys have girlfriends now so it's really nothing to worry about. I find myself being treated as the little girl who needs looking after everywhere I go here. By men that is. It's ok though, the bar manager gave me a ride home last night for nothing; he even offered. I'm told he usually charges $. Seriously- I'm beginning to believe I'm the baby of the family even though you're younger. Never yet had a situation I couldn't handle though. Thank God!

Sandy and Brenda have boyfriends now. I thought Sandy never would! Just about time for last call here but there's always some jerk who comes in at 11:45 and orders 2 or 3 and stays right til 1:00. As long as I can lock up it's ok though. Not a helluva lot else to say except that you better take it easy on dad or I'll come down there and stick up for him, poor dear. Write me. See ya at Xmas for sure. Maybe I'll even come down with Doug for a couple of days if I can swing it. Kinda doubt it though. I'm so tired I could ramble on forever here, but I won't.

Love ya and miss ya lots<br>Rosanne

# Notes: August 1977

THIS MUST HAVE BEEN HER FIRST MOVE AWAY FROM HOME BECAUSE SHE was only nineteen. She was writing from Edmonton, Alberta. She had run off with a black fellow who our family never even met and knew nothing about. The relationship lasted a very short time. She left him and moved in with two very good friends of hers from back home who were sisters. They were all sharing a one-bedroom apartment, which was not ideal.

Graham and the Wilsons were our neighbors, who she disapproves of for being too normal. She admonishes me for lecturing her like Mother. This was an ongoing theme in our lives. Mum and I tended to see eye to eye about everything and it drove Rosanne mad. She hated it when I offered the same advice as Mum. She would always put me in my place and tell me to stop. After all, she was the big sister, and I should respect that. As we grew older, this became more and more of an issue, as she deviated further and further from a path I could condone.

In this letter, she has found a job in a bar, and it sounds like the staff are being really kind to her. There were no doubt men hitting on her constantly because she was very pretty. Good thing she knew how to handle herself. She always knew when someone was trying to take advantage of her, like the customer trying to rip her off. With her wild spirit and cavalier attitude about sex with strangers, it's a miracle that she never got raped. At least she never reported any such scary situation to me. It's a testament to her judgment of people, she had good intuition about who was safe and who was bad news.

    She was meeting up with her old boyfriend Doug, who she calls a doormat because he was passive in nature and would always follow her lead. I don't think she ever did move in with him. She just didn't love him enough to take that leap. He was always a sidepiece to her, poor guy. He must have been smitten to follow her around the country like that.

# Summer 1982

## Letter from home to me in the Yukon

Dear Naomi,

Sorry I didn't get up to see you off dear, but I wasn't home. I crashed at Leah's. Understand the good-byes are too much for me anyhow. The enclosed is a relevant current events clipping (a Bloom County cartoon of a cool looking dude with a penguin and a porcupine on his lap racing downhill towards a humongous walrus). I hope you will appreciate I am getting a new head gasket tomorrow!! Very exciting for me; looking forward to it a lot! I have to go to work now. Bye. Do you love me? Do you care?

Mom's watching Rockford Files.
*Dad has piles.
You're just miles away.
Love Rosanne

*tedious, highly irrelevant clap-trap

# Notes: Summer 1982

I HAD TAKEN OFF FOR THE SUMMER TO LIVE AND WORK IN THE YUKON. She sounds like she feels abandoned by me. "Do you love me? Do you care?" She says that saying good-bye was too much for her, so she let me leave without showing up. This warms my heart, even now.

I guess she really did love me after all, at least at this time in our lives.

# July 1982
## Yukon: Letter from Home

(back of the envelope she wrote:
A big fat letter in honor of all things thick and fat. Yum. Please note stamp.)

Dear Nam,

Just read your letter. Susan was over yesterday with her letter from you and is coming to stay with me Aug.6 when ma and pa go to Hawaii for 2 weeks. I'm a little down right now because I know Mack is going home (to Ontario) pretty soon and, I guess, even though I said I wouldn't, I've become all too fond of him. He's been living here for a week already because Gord wasn't feeding him, and I couldn't afford to so our wonderful parents have conceded to foot the tab so to speak till he can get home. All he has to do is pay the (driving) fine and he can transfer the rest east. We are even allowed to sleep together which I will really miss when he's gone. When will I ever learn eh?

Anyhow I talked to John about it all because he kept phoning etc. and he says that after Mack's gone, he wants me to move to

Kamloops. Satisfied with John after Mack? I doubt it. I'm a silly mixed up kid. I really miss you a lot because you are my sister and would understand why I'm looking after Mack. All my other friends, Leah included, are upset because as he lives here, we do everything together and because I'm being used, to the extreme I might add. I want to do it. I just told him you only get what you give and one day something great will come my way. He would never understand. If not for me though nobody would be there for him and as he said would probably steal a car and head east with nothing. Do you see why? Gord, Dean and Dave (his older brothers) don't want him around. Gord talked him into staying here because he can't afford and doesn't have the time for him. Poor kid really has got the shittiest family. He cried a couple of times for his friends etc. I wished I never met him but couldn't turn him away. I do go on, but I need to I guess.

I do relate to the not your turf stuff, but I'm surprised that you're worried what people here will think if you come home early (from the Yukon). Friends are friends and we all make mistakes, eh? No loss of face involved. Straight goods. It would be excellent if you were back when Mack leaves. I will need a shoulder or three to cry on. I wonder if you missed me this much when I was in Edmonton. Different time and space I suppose. I want a Tundra t-shirt too please or something funky, a conversation piece.

Rosanne's question...How's the sex? I am proud to announce that I can have Mack growling and cumming in 5 minutes now and my leg muscles are very appreciative. I have a hickey on my face and a sore shoulder from falling in the hold of the boat and wrestling. It's a moon age daydream oooh yeah aye. See how this letter cheers up - talking to you is like having a shower (it's not a riddle) cleansing like eh.

Gord came this morning and took little brother for the day - I need the aloneness- bad. He had the nerve to call his wife back east and paid mom for it. Quite a guy. No real news I guess. I only see that family so I don't talk about much else.

I like my job now and they like me enough to give me Tracy's job full-time so at least I have something for me. Glad to hear that you are

## Naomi Lane

working. We can do anything they want can't we? Luck and talent. Neither- fancy is a good word. Well I am starting to ramble a little here so I guess I'll let you go. I'm sorry this letter lacks imagination and I can't really enclose a fart but I'm thinking of you especially when I have to go to the bathroom. Funny that. Mom wants to know if you have Sweet (suite) Modale with you (flute music) or rather just wants her name in this letter- 2 cents as it were.

Just love Yah,<br>Rosanne

PS Any old spoon is ok, but my t-shirt has to have a scoop neck and cap sleeves. Just thought I'd mention it.

(Tiny drawing included of a Player's Light cigarette captioned, "It's what I live for".)

# Notes: July 1982

I AM TOUCHED BY HOW AFFECTIONATE THIS LETTER IS TOWARDS ME. I guess we were really close at this time in our lives, and she confided in me more than anyone else because I understood her and didn't pass judgment on her relationship foibles during this time. I would become more critical as we both got older, which no doubt drove her away.

Rosanne took in eighteen-year-old Mack like he was a stray dog when his own large family refused to support him. She was close with his whole family, including three big brothers, one of whom was married to Leah, her best friend. They were all big men and a roughnecked bunch of party animals from Ontario. It's quite amazing how our parents let him stay in the basement with her for weeks that summer, feeding him and putting up with their sexual escapades downstairs. Rosanne fell in love hard for him and was a mess when he left.

It's also amusing that she has another man waiting in the wings who wants her to move in with him in Kamloops. John was the brother of Monique, another close friend since elementary school. Their family of five had been friends with ours for years and their mother was also British, and they were quite an intellectual and artistic bunch. Rosanne had been seeing John off-and-on before Mack appeared on the scene.

He would visit her whenever he came to Vancouver. I had no idea he was so smitten until I read this letter.

She sounds positive about work and is looking forward to being promoted to a full-time position at her bar job. Rosanne always had a serious work ethic. She almost never called in sick, was hard-working, and enjoyed talking to customers. She made solid friends with her co-workers wherever she went because of her no-nonsense attitude and open disdain for most bosses. I'm sure she was funny and made everyone laugh with her antics.

Her aside about Mum needing to be mentioned in the letter is such a cute observation. I would have never considered how our parents felt in this way. It shows a certain empathy towards them which I did not possess until I was much older.

I forgot she had a spoon collection at this time. How bizarre for a young woman in her early twenties. It seems like more of a hobby for old ladies. I don't know what possessed her to start this, possibly a gift from a relative in Europe? I will never know.

# July 1983

## Ottawa

Dear Naomi,

I know last summer you wrote to me special so I figured I'd better do the same. How are you? We finally rented an apartment. It is nice but we had to say only one of us would be living there and not let on about the dog. I hope nothing goes wrong. We only, or rather, I only want it for about two months so we should be ok. I guess the downstairs (it's part of an old house) has a kitchen, living room, bathroom and one bedroom. Then off the living room up some stairs is what's supposed to be the den. This has a fireplace and nice big windows. I'm letting Wanda have the big room cause I'm working nights and need to sleep in the dark if summer ever comes.

Actually, the weather broke and it's very nice out now. The job I have now is a very nice little bar/deli (only sand and fries etc.) across from Lansdowne Park. You get football players and everything for customers. I am the bartender and am tapping draft quite well surprisingly.

I find Ottawa pretty easy to figure out after driving around for three weeks and apartment hunting. I hate it. The people are all outwardly friendly but there is something intangibly gross about the whole affair. I think I'm a bit lonely. Wanda, like so many Virgos, is a real Susan type and makes me wanna puke a lot. I'm dying to have a belch and a fart competition or hang a moon or bathe in spaghetti. Mack is in his usual financial state (look who's talking) so I talked to him twice on the phone and I guess when we move into the apartment he (and maybe Gord but I hope not) will come and visit for a while. I hope he has enough cash to feed and drink himself.

I'm beginning to feel like what I really came out here for was to see if we really, really had anything, but I miss old Bob and when I talk to Mack I wonder if maybe the whole thing is my little fantasy. He did, however, express how wild it would be to see me and chatted away.

The other job I had was at Len's Deli in the new Rideau Centre cooking fries and stuff but the Jew lady Frida was only there one day and I quit. Her brother Dominic, who hired me, understood when I saw him and had promised to find me something in another of his businesses. He said, "Come and see me," so I was, nearly every day. He's always busy, busy, busy and knows simply everyone in Ottawa so I figured he'd be good to be in with. As it turns out I got a job and apartment on my own but Dominic has been kind enough to pay for my motel room this week and although I drew the line here, asked me if I needed any spending money. This of course is the part you don't tell mom, dad or Bob about. I think he likes me if you know what I mean. I haven't seen him since I moved in but I'm sure the catch is coming and I feel that in the interest of a few hundred bucks I can handle it. Who needs to walk the streets, all you have to do is smile. Sick eh. Oh well, a little attention goes a long way in these desperate times and if Bob had coughed up I wouldn't have to prostitute my affections eh. Hopefully he'll pay for another week and a half until we move, but who knows.

I'm all by myself in the city and I miss my car. Wanda is staying in Hawkesbury, thank god. I'd definitely be paying my own way otherwise. I really can't wait to get this summer over with and I hope that if I do see Mack that it doesn't eat at me for months afterwards like last time but I can't resist temptation as I probably should in this case. I dream about him every night. Last night he hated me and I made a fool of myself but sometimes it's nice.

I hear you saw Chris. How did that go? Anything there? Isn't it awful how important men are to us? I'm sure if I had a man out here I'd be fine but right now I'm a little blue. I think I'm actually writing this letter more for my benefit than yours. I needed someone to talk to. All I've been doing for a month is running around Ottawa like a chicken with its head cut off.

I have to call someone at U.I. (unemployment insurance) pretty soon and after we move. I'm going to start my volunteering so it looks like every moment of my summer will be filled with shit I hate, like work and Wanda. Oh well, it will be over soon. I sorta hope some crisis like Auntie Fry coming over (from England) occurs so I have to come home but then I can't afford that either I guess. It would take a long time to transfer my U.I. back again (to BC). It hasn't even got here yet. Anyway, enough drivel. Write me. I'll give mom my new address on the phone where I'll be after June 1st. Take care eh.

Love, Rosanne

# July 1983: Notes

THIS LETTER IS FILLED WITH HOMESICKNESS AND LONELINESS. SHE IS discovering at age 24 that leaving home to make it on your own is harder than it looks. She half admits that she moved across the country to chase the eighteen-year-old Mack who she fell in love with during the previous summer in BC. This is unlikely to work out because of their age difference and, at that time, he was back home with his parents in another Ontario town and is flat broke. It's awful that she was dreaming every night about making a fool of herself over him. She knew deep down that it would never work.

She also still feels connected to Bob, who would eventually get fed up with waiting for her, sell her car that she left behind, and keep the money she so desperately needed. There is an unending disappointment that seemed to follow her wherever she went.

She tells me not to tell our parents that some Jewish businessman is now paying her way and finding her employment in return for sexual favors. She admits that this is easier than walking the streets turning tricks to get ahead. In fact, she later told our parents about this relationship and was quite proud of how savvy she had been to find a rich man to take care of her.

I remember Mum explaining this to me and shaking her head. Like with all Rosanne's bold moves, I think Mum secretly admired her chutzpah and wished she could have lived such a daring life. I don't think Mum worried about her safety; she always believed that Rosanne could handle herself. Dad would have rolled his eyes and said something glib, but he would have secretly been more worried. If he had ever answered the phone, he would have given her a good talking to, and she would have felt ashamed.

It's too bad her friendship with Wanda wasn't more mutual because Wanda really did make an effort to help her. Rosanne found her too uptight but agreed to live with her because she was alone and didn't know anyone else. It also benefits her to share the rent. They did end up keeping in touch for many years after she moved back home so Rosanne grew to appreciate Wanda, given more time and distance.

I don't recall what volunteering she did, but she is evidently setting up her unemployment insurance just in case her new job doesn't pan out. She sounds worried that this will tie her to Ottawa for longer than she wanted. She already sounds ready to come back home after just a few months. She finds the people outwardly friendly but inwardly fake. I remember her talking about all the federal civil servants coming into her bar in their business attire. This was not her usual crowd, but she would adapt like a chameleon, as she always did so well. Anything for the tips. She explained that there was a large contingency of gay men working in the government offices and she made at least one close friend among them. She got a real kick out of dressing up and going to drag bars with him on her nights off.

It was a rough start, but she did manage to stay in Ottawa for a couple of years and find her feet as an independent young woman, until everything fell apart. I am touched by this letter because it's clear that she really valued our connection during this difficult time.

# August 1983

## Ottawa

(Envelope addressed to Young Buck)

Dear Naomi P,

You asked for a letter so here it is. I'm having a lazy day today. Wanda and Donny are both at work and I did exercises instead of swimming- to David's Aladdin Sane. Think he meant "a lad insane" there or what? I do. Never thought about it before.

Susan called yesterday to announce that she is working and will most likely stay until November and then go to work at Whistler. Watch Betty (her mother) overdose eh!

When are you going to stop wasting your life taking courses you can't do or won't do you any good? Be a drop-out-work for a living, live a little, make some sense for christ's sake. Listen to big sister, having your shit together isn't everything- if it was I would be non-existent- no more- passed on- this bird is dead- finished etc. Anyways.

I have a totally different lifestyle here than what I'm used to, as would figure I suppose. I start my day at 5:45 am by getting up and making Donny coffee and a lunch. We smoke a J if we have one-then an hour later I go back to bed- get up again at 10- go swimming- Wanda comes if she's on nights or I go alone. After that I either do shopping or run little errands-make Donny supper and go to work. He is always asleep when I get home so I don't see him much except Saturday and all day Sunday. There now. Monday I start a day shift job and I took Saturday off this weekend so things will improve, but for a month yet I think I'll have to work two jobs; at least for football games and concerts and the exhibition days. What- miss part time- but two jobs- wild but true.

Weighing 140 even these days I can't believe it myself eh. Don't feel any different though. Was thinking of Mark today. He never even called after the weekend he was here. Oh well, probably best I guess.

Did I tell you the Roughriders, or some of them, come after practice at my work. You have never seen such huge and handsome men! One black guy is always extremely nice to me and I figure if I did stay there he'd ask me out sooner than later. I wonder if I'd go. Donny would never ever understand-he'd flip out on me. But this guy is like Mr. Fucking Wonderful eh. Not that I ever have a free weekend to do anything anyways. Last weekend Donny went out Friday and Saturday while I worked and then on Sunday we had no money to do anything but little angel-woman, me, said nothing like a fool.

This time we're going to his dad's cottage I think. Did y'all get the story of the car? No? Well...Donny borrowed Wanda's car to go to the bank one eve. He's not insured. He goes up on a curb to avoid a swerving taxi. He breaks the upper control arm. We waste two weekends getting it fixed at our expense. We all start to be bitchy a lot. Yes I told you the last of it is being done today thank god. I'm the middle person in this three's-a-crowd sit-com. Rose, Donny this- Rose, Wanda that eh. Who gives a fuck eh? What do I care if the two of them meet fisties while I'm at work. I told them that if this was to be another car weekend that I was off to Hell solo.

It's now 7 am Wed. morning and I'm here cooking pickerel (fresh) and potatoes in the oven for Donny's supper. I work two shifts today so it's now or never. I'm tired, I work the same tomorrow- I'll be tired then too. I bought a Melita coffee maker in preparation for all this.

We had a pretty good weekend at the coddige (cottage). Nothing amazing-lots of kids around all the time, I like that. Food waitressing (I started that yesterday) is not so bad. The tips are better and I suppose I'll get used to it eh. Lebanese own all restaurants here and are considered as lovely as Sikhs in BC only they're not dirty. My new boss seems ok though. So much to remember with food. Can I handle it?

Was a full moon weekend and how. All was well until Sunday night and I was ok but Donny cried for an hour-I felt like mom-saying "it's a full moon don't be silly" etc. Am I growing up? Eeek! No no I don't want to!!

Coffee; pas de cum. Lebanese, to the best of my knowledge, pick strawberries. Saturday evening now-must finish later. Job much better as time goes on-food waitressing is just a different routine, that's all. Gotta start apartment hunting this week for sure. The international organizer from Montreal of the hotel union was talking to Wanda at her place(non-union) and she mentioned my unfortunate situation about no union work. He asked my name and remembered me from being in the Ottawa office at the same time I guess. He gave her his card for me and said I can call him collect. I'd move to Montreal and check it out if it was worth it. More industry in Montreal for Donny too eh (a welder). I'll call him Tuesday morning for sure. Never a dull moment eh!

Anyways take care and phone me when you can afford it. Letters are getting hard to write for me lately so it's no reflection on you if the next one takes a while ok. I love mail so keep up the chatter out there girls- talk it up- let's go now! Compare letters with Bev if you want- one off to her simultaneous eh. Beryl and Cindy can wait another week.

Wish you were here. Will see Margot (Mother's friend) for dinner and a flick Monday or Tuesday. I ain't had one nice dinner out since I left BC so let's hope she's buyin'- kidding. Getting real brown (proud of myself here) how bout yous? Tell ma I never took any photos away but I sure wouldn't mind a few. Cried a little when I got the one of her and your letter had me crying and laughing at the same time-no real outbursts though for some time (am I really growing up?) Tweet tweet as our dear dad would say.

See ya later<br>
Love ya much<br>
Rosanne

# Notes: August 1983 Ottawa

SHE WAS GOING THROUGH ONE OF HER EXERCISING PHASES, WHICH normally involved swimming, but aerobics was just becoming a huge industry at this time, so it was not unusual to dance around the house doing exercises too. Weighing 140 pounds was a record low for us girls. Mother always said we had "big bones" which was just a nice way of denying that our whole family tended to be fat if we didn't work out a lot. The exercise made her more stable for sure by helping elevate her mood, as it does for all of us.

She would routinely encourage me to stop wasting my time at university learning about completely useless things. She wanted me to get a job and slug it out in the real world like she was. This wasn't out of jealousy or meanness; she really believed that I would be better off working. She felt like I was living a fake elitist existence at university that was out of touch with reality. In truth, she felt intimidated by that whole environment. University was like our father taking us to a Board of Trade luncheon and trying to marry us off to some businessman in a suit. She loathed the whole idea.

You can see that she spends a lot of her time doting on Donny and making his meals. Why she didn't dump his ass and run off with the handsome Ottawa Roughrider is beyond me. It sounds like she has the perfect opportunity. Gosh, he even made more money than Donny. He might have taken her out on the weekend, instead of spending all his wages getting drunk with other people while she was busting her hump working two jobs! What an asshole. She deserved so much better.

She had started working for Lebanese restaurant owners and compares them to the Sikhs in Vancouver. There was rampant racism against the Indian population when they first started joining our schools in the 1980's, hence her shameful remark about them being dirty. She also doubts her abilities to remember the food menu, which surprises me. She usually thought she was smarter than everyone else in the room.

It's so ironic that she spent an hour comforting a crying Donny during the full moon, which had always affected her terribly. How the tables had turned. Apparently, she had found a man who was as emotionally stable as she was.

At the end of the letter, she asks poignantly, "Am I really growing up?" Of course, she was. It was her first time so far away from home and seeing the photo of Mum inside the letter made her cry. She was becoming an independent woman while feeling homesick as well. Leaving home was liberating but hard. Her support network consisted of one female friend, Wanda, who often annoyed Rosanne and Donny, who offered nothing in terms of emotional or financial support.

I think she felt very alone.

# Late August 1983

Dear Naomi,

    A yellow page to reflect your ever sunny disposition- how fitting. Susan came to see me at the latest job the other day -she promised to show me her ten-pager so you can relax on that subject for um...a week. Lovely touch, the Donny edition of the Naomi letter. He's not home yet but I'm sure it will warm his heart as does any attention. The poor little blighter. It were him's birfday last Friday and I got him stuff and genuinely surprised him with it in the morning before he went to work. He went to his dad's cottage for the weekend and one sister got him a boring card and everyone else apparently had no idea it was his birthday or even how old he was. Sad eh. His big brother-in-law says "no Donny" and the opposite of whatever he says and does all the time-so much that I nearly cried. I was so fed up with it. I wouldn't take it and it sickens me that Donny feels it's best to ignore it-I'd like to tell the fuckhead to suck shit, which no doubt I will one of these fine days. His dad caught on and assured me I needn't pay any attention to John when he says we owe for a case of beer, to which I replied, "or any other time for that matter," which gave Dad a good chuckle. He likes me I can tell.

    I can feel summer ending here- it's a bit depressing-I'm sleeping too much these past couple of days- a sure sign. We don't get fooled again- the Who. Get on my knees and pray. We are moving on the first eh- I was sweating all about what the hell we were going to do for furniture but lo and be-fucking-hold God really loved us all the time. This lady down the street with a far worse accent than even Margot's, met my Donny and felt he could put to use all her cottage stuff for pennies. I just talked to her on the phone and she'll keep it for us 'til the first and is going to throw in dishes and stuff too. We're getting a beige with red (I love it) oriental rug- a pink (love it) old stuffed chair-lamps-a standing ashtray-a folding table and chairs-a couch (old) and a bed (wow eh). I can't wait to move, I'm so excited about it. I went yesterday and bought pink towels, a pink lace tablecloth and some doilies from the antique store. Fun city! All we need now is a stereo and Wanda's going to check into a hot cassette-deck-radio affair for me. I want my stereo! And records! I need a quilt too- $39.95 at Zellers-no problem. Oh boy, I want my posters too, my camera, pictures and gold bracelet-why can't I have them? They're mine. (I'm serious).

You should be here. Fuck, Wanda and Donny - cute couple- Wanda was snitty last night and Donny just about hit her and she just about called the cops. I closed my eyes, slid off my (sorry Wanda's) chair, and curled up in a corner. I think Wanda should've waited 'til I wasn't around to have it out with him-she knows I don't want anything to do with whatever is between them. Donny says she can't come over to our place ever. I have to borrow her vacuum tho'. Wanda is a fool-all she has to do is stop being so prissy and self-righteous with him. I don't know or care.

My new job is phenomenal-I'm bartending and making $50 in tips a day- wow! Nice place too-all old stone arches etc. Banana daiquiri anyone? Went to the Ex (P.N.E. type affair) last night and this is where they get crazy-a beer garden just packed with "heads"-like the old Cariboo pub. I want to go there again tonight cause we've more money today and I could get into a severe rowdy drunk. I'm going to end up in jail on account of my debts one day, but life is for living not trying to pay things you can't pay that's what I say! I tried to borrow two grand from the bank, so I'd only have one payment monthly, but they laughed at me so fuck them all! Anyway, Donny will be home soon so I'm going to get beautiful. See you in the movies, you stereo-thieving, pyromaniacal, incestuous, spineless, monstrous pig you.

Love Rosanne

# Notes: Late August 1983

IT'S TOUCHING HOW PROTECTIVE SHE IS OF DONNY'S FEELINGS AROUND his family. She will always stick up for the underdog when there's any kind of condescending meanness going on. I think she feels this to her core because she always felt like the underdog in our family and in the world at large. I'm surprised she didn't have a verbal go at big brother John, but it was the first time meeting them after all. She probably wanted to make a good first impression. At least the old father saw her and appreciated her candor and wit.

Money was always an issue and it's nice that this total stranger stepped up to provide them with furniture. You can hear how much she enjoys home decorating, especially with pink decor and little antique finds. This woman truly helped her out of a depressing situation and gave her a creative outlet at the same time.

She often complained of her friend Wanda acting too prissy with her partner. I'm not sure if "prissy" meant that Wanda was strong and authoritative. Rosanne was definitely the opposite with her men. She turned into this passive, mothering wifey thing that I could not recognize. Then at other times, she would flip her switch and let them have a blast of her sarcasm and temper. One of her friends recently asked me if she was bipolar. I'm not sure why her doctors kept referring to her condition as a mood disorder rather than bipolar, but there seems to be little distinction between the two terms. This would really help to explain why she had these two radically different personas around her men. It's so strange to me how she feels the need to get all dolled up with make-up whenever Donny is coming home from work. This "little woman" persona flies in the face of the sister I knew, who was strong and feisty. Why did she feel the need to impress this short, dirty man in welder's coveralls who did nothing in return for her? Was her self-esteem really so low that she feared him leaving if she wasn't sexy enough?

She is ready to go back to the EX (exhibition) beer garden and get her drink on, fueled by the banks laughing in her face when she tried to consolidate her debt, which was a relatively new concept at this time. I suppose her income looked low because she couldn't prove to them that she was making large tips on top of her salary. It sounds like the whole interaction made her feel small and she needed to blow off some steam.

# September 1983

## Birthday Card from Ottawa

On the Front: Happy Birthday Sister

>You're so damn cute
>Just like this card
>You make me puke
>You little retard
>You are my sister
>You are my friend
>To you my dear
>My love I send
>The end. Again.
>Rosanne

>So sorry this is your present. I'll make it up to you one fine day

# September 1983

Envelope addressed to Percy Nympholina Cressenda-written Sept.23/83 a significant date (her birthday)-sent whenever I can afford a stamp

Dear Nirobi (XLax for short),

You will notice the caffeine stain on this page. You may get a question or two on it later. It is personalization of sorts- an insignia. Tacky card-or is it just me? Nice little verse tho'- extremely appropriate. The tights too, were appropriate. Speaking of hair, mine was quite long. I went to get my bangs only trimmed the other day. Three inches later. Coulda killed 'er. Silly goose if so. Yours must be pull men up the castle walls length by now. Yes, cut it. Gloat, gloat.

See, if I was home, you wouldn't even think about it would you? So Don the man took off ce matin pas avec wishing moi a happy birthday. Oh well, I got stuff from you all and Brian, my gay friend, took me to lunch the other day. Wanda made me some cushions (very nice) and Susan the great (great what? I don't know) is coming to pay me a birthday visit this evening after work (also very nice and thoughtful). All in all life ain't bad eh.

I got myself all dolled up after swimming today just to make myself feel good. I'm wearing my purple with little burgundy flowers flannelette skirt and top with mom's exquisitely funky sweater. I did my hair up and perfumed and painted myself into another world. Heaven, to be exact.

Donny is happy whenever he gets home. Whenever does not mean I don't know when he'll be home; in this house "whenever" is used exactly like "when" is at your house, see. Shhh, I don't have anything for supper for Susan or Donny. Why should I? Hehe. Dig it? I myself am not hungry. Quite a change for me lately. Nearly fucking died at swimming today. Miss purple tomato head after; you know. I'm considering ladies' rhythmic fitness Tues. and Thurs. evenings. It's only just around the corner, as is swimming eh. Eh, eh, I must be going deaf or sumping eh. Oooh, I dunno. I have also got my name down for some weaving classes at a little shop near here. Once I remember everything, I'll get a small loom.

Guess what's for Xmas? For Donny we are getting CABLEVISION! Oh no! I had a week almost off here and I can't wait to start working again. Only so much you can do with no bucks, no car eh. The old apartment is starting to look sorta normal. I guess I probably told you already about my pink chesterfield cover up for $3. I got a few dried flowers, Wanda's cushions and some Renoir mini-prints as well as Indian corn, which looks nice on the wall. I have the boat party Renoir one as well as another of a couple waltzing in a bar with background people and beer. Very nice also. Our bedroom remains empty except for the token cat picture and one of a Swedish winter window with table below on which sits a horse like the orange painted wooden one on ma's dresser. Need an extra bed. I hate to think I can't accommodate visitors even tho', or however unlikely I am to have any.

So my dear, thank you so kindly and with a slight air, or ear, of reverence for the stockings. Take good care of your sickly self and don't fly too close to the sun. After all, we are merely flesh and bloody bone eh.

> Love and a great deal of necessary tolerance,
> Your aged sibling or sister or sublime sibling, Rosanne

# Notes: September 1983

THIS LETTER IS INCREDIBLY SAD TO ME. SHE IS IN LOVE WITH A MAN who cannot even remember or acknowledge her fucking birthday. She has to doll herself up after her morning swim just to make herself feel happier. It's like some sad actor putting on their own makeup backstage before facing the audience. I want to punch this Donny in the face when I read this, but he is already dead and so is she.

She finds her own happiness in making herself more beautiful, exercising, decorating her home, and finding little objets d'art for the walls. She is creative and frugal. I love that she is wanting to get a loom and get back into weaving. All these activities are healthy outlets for an otherwise frustratingly broke existence. It speaks volumes that she can't handle a week off without getting bored because her partner can't even hold an interesting conversation, never mind spending two cents to take her out anywhere. Their relationship always seemed purely sexual. She said he was good in bed. There was nothing otherwise redeeming about him.

In all her years of chasing men, she never once referred to a man pleasuring her to ecstasy, but perhaps she only talked to her girlfriends about this. Instead, she often expressed how well she pleasured them or how fast she could make them cum. I just hope she received as much pleasure as she gave and didn't spend her life in sexual frustration.

Poverty is the other running theme of her letters. Cablevision is the great purchase of the year and a three-dollar pink chesterfield cover obviously made her very happy. She always worked hard to provide, and I never once had a sense that her partners were hard-working in any relationship other than the truck driver, who seemed to have money. She set the bar so incredibly low. She believed to her core that poor people were her flock and she belonged with them. Anything else would have been snobbery. I don't know where she got this notion from. Perhaps it was Dad's upbringing in a wealthy Jewish family in Frankfurt that disgusted her. He had servants and nannies as a child, but lost everything in the Holocaust, including his parents. I don't know why she would have framed her identity in opposition to his childhood riches.

It's strange because our parents were just average middle class immigrant workers. We always had enough, but nothing fancy. It was as if she rejected everything about our family life to prove a point. Mother would say that she "cut off her nose to spite her face". She could have done so much better than these low life selfish, lazy men.

# Fall 1983

## Ottawa

Dear Nam,

 I know you're probably swamped with mid-terms etc. so I decided to write you a letter so you don't run short of reading material eh. I was surprised to hear that you thought I should stay here; I figured you'd say I should go to school right away. I know my car is ok at Bob's for a while but I would like to have it here, or at least out of there before the winter. See I told him I'd just stay 'til winter but of course this wasn't true eh. Of course, it would be nice to leave it there for a bit yet cause he says he's still gonna fix the rear brakes for me sometime soon.

 Anyways that is really the only problem, major like, that I have in life at the moment. My boss was hating me but not talking about it, thus I was hating her, so the other night I went to her and said, "Look, we have to either sort this thing out or forget it." We had a long talk and now we understand where one another is coming from way better, but I'm still gonna see the personnel manager at the hotel again Monday to try for a day shift job. He remembered me when I called so maybe if I'm real sugar sweet we can work something out.

 As for Dominic, fuck it. I was only fond of him I think because he helped me out a lot when the chips were down at first but I really need someone with more time for just me and someone more my type. Dominic thinks that everyone who is not prestigious is an idiot, including me sometimes and he has tantrums about stupid ass things like dirt spots on his Mercedes. I mean really come on. I flat out stood him up more than once lately, so if he really wants me maybe he'll make a big effort, otherwise that's that I'm afraid. Money is nice but time and love and attention, like, are more important to me I guess.

When you called I mentioned that Donny was here, well, Donny has time for me eh and he's as good in the sack as any of Mack's brothers you'd care to mention. A little shorter than me eh, and a throw together of Dougie D, Willy W, and Shortie only with a bit more savvy than any of the above. Some of the Doug similarities are for sure. It's like they look at things the same way. I never ever understood Doug well until after the fact but the lesson was learned and really all it was was a need for a lot of attention but an "I don't need it" front. Very caring people too really only you must trust them. Ramble ramble ramble eh. Donny proposed to me, night before last, and said the end of August would be nice but who knows eh.

He's supposed to be here now but isn't but I think he's paying me back for last night when I went to Hell (nightclub) after work with this girl and didn't come home until 4 am. Not pleased eh. No we're not living in but we stay at each other's place every night. Sure nice to have that freedom again after so long at home.

My skin is all peeling off and it's so itchy. I'm sure you of all people can identify with the way I feel about my stereo. It's like I'm being ripped off- I paid for it monthly for 3 years and now you have it free- not fair. How will you ever repay me? Selfish eh- have to be a bit in life or be walked on all the time like I used to be. Touch of self pity here sorry but it's 1 am and I'm sleepy I guess. Hard day at the office.

Hope Brenda does come out here for a while. I think we're going to see about a big house and rent bedrooms, me Wanda, Donny and if Susan and Adam decide to stay (haven't even mentioned it to her yet) them too. Who knows, just a thought really. Oh - weight-wise eh-145 pounds and holding thanx. Hair gray but long-outlook positive. Wars of the world unleash your wrath upon me for I am woman, I am strong, I am invincible, but I am not, thank God, Helen Reddy eh. My boss is.

I haven't wrote Lydia yet to tell her I'm staying; her last letter (after birthday card) asked what bullshit this was, me staying out here. She will not be pleased. Perhaps I should send her a nice shrubbery with a stream running through it to sooth the bash a bit eh. But then what if she had no pockets, it would be awkward to carry around eh. Sacré men (sacrement), calisse, tabernac, hostie, ba- tow (bateau) là, ma nouvelle vocabulaire là.

Never did hear from Don (Vancouver) , wonder how he's doing these days. I wrote Johnny a letter. Wonder if he'll write back. I don't get enough mail, like fuck all yous, I ain't writing no more til I get a little appreciation. It's me stuck out here alone not vice-versa eh. Brenda writes but it's nonsense with pictures of naked bucks etc. Not that I don't like nonsense you understand it's just bloody nonsense that's all. Bye- going to quit this nonsense and crash now. May the sun shine up your rectum and out your ears and (heaven forbid) nose dear.

Sister dearest, yours, R.

An additional remarque or two here. I got a call from Bob - ce matin et il est moving house so I have about 2 weeks to get my car out of there- can some dear old soul out there afford to get it towed to Brenda's if I promise to pay back after? (Just send me a bill for it ok, ok. I guess he's moving to Fort Langley and I guess he's not telling anyone but the family exactly where eh. Typical pout bout, but I guess he's on bad terms with his dad etc cause he told him to get on with things instead of crying over me all the time. Poor old Bob- a true-to-form fuck up through and through. He and Lydia are in communique. So I'll hear more about it yet. Lydia has a new beau I hear too, which is good cause celibacy is no more her bag than mine and it's been 3-4 months now-a record for the little red-haired girl. Anyhow I'm now extra-curious as to whether or not Brenda would consider driving the great white out or not. The keys, by the way, will be in the glove box and her tapes, my piggy-bank and present from Bob's dad's trip to Reno will be in the car too. Sorry for this inconvenience and all but what can I say eh. Keep me posted already.

Much love (heaps of it),
Rosanne E. Schreiber

# Notes: Ottawa Fall 1983

Even though Rosanne rarely dated her letters, this one was obviously written at the end of summer because her skin is peeling from too much sun exposure. She is sounding more settled in her new city now, with a job and some connections. She says that she lied to her ex-boyfriend Bob about coming back to Vancouver by winter. He is apparently pining after her and she is still hoping to get a brake job out of him before she dumps him, which would seem only fair to her.

I am impressed that she was trying to make peace with the boss woman at work. It shows some real maturity that she initiates this peace talk, considering that she is most likely much younger than her boss. The outcome was positive, and they reached some kind of understanding. I seldom saw this kind of diplomacy on Rosanne's part. Perhaps as she grew older, she had less patience for other people's bullshit or perhaps her mental illness made it more difficult. She would have more feuds with bosses as the years passed.

She is in the process of ending things with another sugar-daddy Dominic, who she is tired of sleeping with to get ahead. Rosanne couldn't stand pretentious people, so when she says that Dominic thinks prestige and intelligence are synonymous, that means she was beginning to hate him for looking down his nose at her. If there's one thing Rosanne hated, it was being called stupid. She was definitely sharp as a tack when it came to reading people, other than the men she was sleeping with that is.

At this point, she was just entered a new relationship with Don, whose main asset is being good in the sack. She describes him as needing a lot of attention, pouting when he doesn't get it, and out to get revenge for her coming home so late the previous night. What excellent qualities for the future father of your children! They are considering moving in together because they are already sleeping at each other's places every night anyhow.

It's funny that she expects ex-boyfriends to write her letters. I have never known, in the history of the universe, any ex-boyfriend to write any ex-girlfriend a letter. This is a strange notion, but I guess she still sees all her ex-boyfriends as friends. No hard feelings, right?

I feel bad that she wants her stereo sent out there after making three years of payments to purchase it. Electronics were so expensive back in the seventies! Perhaps our parents didn't want to pay for shipping those heavy albums across the country? I cannot remember, although I was certainly the beneficiary of them being left behind.

She asks us to rescue her car from Bob's quickly because he is moving. Why didn't we do this for her? I really don't know. I remember that Bob lived far outside the city in the more rural part of the Fraser Valley in a trailer. This would have been an expensive tow truck charge for our parents for sure. They may have attempted it but were too late because he sold it out from under her and her possessions in the back seat were never recovered either. This was a huge loss for Rosanne, who couldn't afford another vehicle for several years afterwards. She was really devastated when he pocketed the cash. It was an unforgivable transgression from a man we had all loved and trusted. I even remember my dad being disappointed in him.

# December 1983
## Ottawa

(Tiny Xmas card with a cow on the front (sent from Ottawa to Naomi E. because she called me Edwina)

Mooy Xmas Nam

Found this fella
He'd strayed far
Asked where you are
So not another word
I'll send you to rejoin the herd
All the other nerds
Music to my ears said he
Moosic that will play for me
Corn fed eh.

# Spring 1984
## Ottawa

Hello, this is Sunday, what's that? My mom called me this morning. It was nice. She says I'm getting my stereo, how very permanent. I get the weekend off this time. Don has gone fishing and has taken the truck to Bourgette to get it fixed for cheap. I went to the spring festival and had Debbie and Karen for breakfast yesterday. Today I'm cleaning out my cupboards for the pest control and doing laundry, floors, vacuuming, sorting, and packing of wearables and generally fucking the dog's left ear. So to speak. You?

I hear you may be coming early and Brenda is going to come almost for sure. I hope I can be fun enough to have made it worth your whiles and compensate for Don's probable bad humors. You know how Dad is when Auntie Betty has been around for a week or so. I look forward to being told to shut up in front of my friends, who wouldn't? I must be the envy of my hometown.

Mom is a lucky woman. She alone shares my auto-notary pleasures. Gives one's middle finger that sleek, exercised, well cared for appearance eh. See how the paper appears mutilated? It is.

Don just came home a day early and we had a little dispute, which I lost. So that was a few hours ago and lover is now snoring on the couch after we had our feed of fresh fish and chips and a roll in the sack. Good fish and chips, we'll have to do some for you while you're here. Good sack too. You don't get any of that, sorry.

I have very little to do myself. How could I share this...shut up I says to myself I says ok. They got fake Indians on the TV but I'm waiting for Ronny Corbet in Sorry and then Monty Python's Flying Circus. I love Sundays for that. And so thinking logically, I think to myself, my wife has been fucking the milkman all the day and now the milkman has gone, so supper will now be made. This, in context with an East Indian accent, is quite amusing. Debbie has a friend who looks quite like John Cleese and does it very well. "Ver is supper, I ask my wife." "I have been fucking the milkman all day and you want supper?" she replied etc.

I had, as I said, to empty all the cupboards, for pest control to come. Well you should've seen Don's face when he came in to see everything stacked up on the table ready to pack like. Surprise is mild, but accurate. He loves me, I can tell. Once in a while.

Sooo anyways, Wanda is still with her boyfriend there and the more she tells me about him the more he sounds as though he has all of Don's worst habits that Wanda hates. Oh well it's funny how you tend to put up with much more when it's your own.

Lydia called on Mom's Day and sounded well, yes, boring. I'll send a little something for her birthday just for the sake of it but we do seem to be losing touch. I think it has something to do with the fact that for once I am more interested in me than in Lydia. She doesn't like that. Of course, time and distance could make me see things in a less than real light. Who knows the answers to these remarkably deep and controversially important questions. Qui cares, as the French here would say.

So dearie, time for the English humor injection grows nigh and I must say see you later. Actually, it's sooner than we think. Very soon in fact. My goosebumps are a 40DD just thinking about it. Gosh I hope this letter was foolish enough. I haven't given you the impression I'm intelligent, have I? The BBC would like to apologize for the following announcement.

> The end.
> Love and kisses (fishy ones)
> Rosanne

Special effects: Beethoven and Rommel's army (not to mention the unmentionable).

# Spring 1984: Notes

It's funny to read her words, "My mom phoned me this morning". She is laying claim to our mother in a charmingly possessive way. She obviously misses her very much.

My visit to see her was imminent that spring and she already sounds embarrassed about me meeting Don. She is also wary of her friend Brenda hating him as well, which she no doubt would have. She says he will be foul tempered like Dad, and she is ashamed of him telling her to shut up in front of her friends. He sounds just lovely. They seem to argue and make up via sex very frequently. They are both hot-headed, which is a recipe for disaster.

Then there are tender moments where she says she knows that he loves her. Ironically, this comes out when she is cleaning for pest control. How romantic! They seem to blow hot and cold. She dotes on him endlessly, cooking and cleaning and preening herself to look good for him. It all makes me sick to my stomach. She observes her friend Wanda doing the same fawning over her man and comments that "it's funny how you put up with so much more when it's your own." She has an unspoken ally to help her justify her lousy relationship.

I'm glad to hear that she had a couple of women over for breakfast. At least she is making some new girlfriends. Her long-time friendship with Lydia seems to be waning, as absence does not make the heart grow fonder in this instance. She is taking stock of their old dynamic, feeling like it was all give and no take. She is going through the motions with her long distance at this point.

I'm not sure what she meant by Mum sharing her auto-notatary pleasures. Is she talking about letter writing or masturbation? It's unclear to me. She could be saying that they both like letter-writing, but it sounds more like they are both left to pleasure themselves because their men don't look after their sexual needs. She has never spoken about herself or Mother in this way, so it took me by surprise. I don't understand her strange comment, "See how the paper appears mutilated?" Is she referring to her genitalia? Is she referring to using her middle finger to masturbate or possibly just flipping her middle finger to say "Fuck off" to the world? This paragraph confuses me.

We shared a love of British comedy shows on TV. They were all so absurd and we would roll off the couch laughing so hard whenever we watched them together. I truly miss this shared sense of humor. Nobody else in my life ever had the same appreciation for the ridiculousness of our parents' relationship, which often seemed so completely absurd that it could have been straight out of Monty Python. There was never any apparent physical affection between them. We never saw them kiss or hug in front of us or call each other affectionate pet names like most couples do. They moved into separate bedrooms when they were fifty. They were almost like the caricature couple of Terry Jones dressed in drag as the wife and Graham Chapman as the oblivious husband. This was our bond as sisters. We could laugh at our own lives together.

# Summer 1984

Envelope addressed to Nirobi Schpelia

Dear Naomi (or whatever the case may be),

Thanx for the at work letter. I'm glad you're having an ok time lately. Sounds like you're just the busiest little bee. Right about now I think it would be very nice to have a couple more friends and family around. Lydia called last night and I wished to see her too. She says she's body-building like her big new man. Bet she looks great and sounds as though she has emerged from the nucleus state that Les had her in (previous relationship).

I hear Susan called you on your birthday- she said you had a good chat. I'm supposed to see her on her break today at 2. Presently I'm having coffee, it's 8 a.m. and my man just left to work after puking his guts out totally. New job today eh. Hypertension city. He says he loves me.

Wanda was busy cleaning every inch of her new place last night when we were there (had to drag Donny). Her pad (new word) is sort of like my old one in New West. Big and high like that. Very, very dirty though. She very much likes it now that it's cleaned up though, as I told her she would. I wish it was mine, unsecretly. I guess our place is wider and slightly less long than the room downstairs there (at home). Not as dull though. The bedroom is as yet uninhabited as we are using a sofa-bed the landlady gave me. I got a white quilt with pink, blue and yellow small bright flowers on it and green grass and leaves around them. I'd really like a camera out here so I could show you these things again (hint hint). Get it. Pass it on. And my perfumes. These are relatively small items, no problem lugging back whenever, if ever, I do return to paradise.

My latest job is ok, good tips, but you run for them quite often. I'm hoping I'll hear from this hospital today. I had an interview with the head cook and personnel last week and I figured it looked pretty good. It's in dietary for about three days a week at $8.50 an hour to start. I can live on that.

I was interrupted for a while here. Wanda and gay Brian, my nurse friend from upstairs, came for coffee. We had cheese, apples, veggie thins and peanut butter. It was fun. I don't get to socialize too much cause Donny is a very possessive man. He doesn't like me to think of anyone but him really, but Brian is no threat because he's gay and did, after all, help us quite a lot lately. It's his god-mom who runs this building we're in, otherwise we'd have been apartment hunting forever. She, as I said, gave us the sofa bed (in the same material as that old couch I had before) and Brian lent us two kitchen chairs for our fold-out table. Don tries to put up with Wanda because he knows I need to have a friend. He doesn't seem to mind Susan at all, but then we don't see much of her. I would really love for you and mom and dad to meet him but I think we'd best wait until our relationship matures a bit before we start to think about moving west. I know he will if I want to, but I think all my acquaintances there would make him jealous and even perhaps ruin things all together. Later, when he knows he can trust me completely and we are a solid couple, this will change I'm sure. It's just a course things have to take I guess. Not that it's shaky, it's just relatively new and we need time to feel each other out. He says we'll get married when we can afford to have everyone together for that and of course a three-thousand-dollar ring for me. Ha ha.

I must repeat myself in each letter, but my whole life revolves around Donny right now so what else do I really have to say eh. He also wants to have children, which is a real bonus. I think it would be good for him to have some responsibilities along those lines cause he likes to be the boss and have attention all the time. Kids would fill gaps for him I'm sure. How do you feel about being an aunt? Would you come and look after me if I need someone around like a post-natal advisor or would my dear mom have to fill this position. I think maybe I'd have to take a course eh. Anyhow, this is all speculatory at present but it's a thought eh.

These snaps I'm enclosing were taken by the infamous Susan about two months ago at Mooney's Bay, an in the city beach on the river near here. We were very, very relaxed, if you get my drift. Please send me one of you and one of dad at least, if not my whole album of stuff.

Gord called me last night to tell me he's leaving his wife forever and going west again soon. I don't know what he thought. Maybe that I'd beg him to take me along and that we'd, at long last, get it together. Anyway, he said he may stop in Ottawa on the way out next week or so. Whatever. I guess Mack, the little gigolo, is shacked up with some 36-year-old woman these days and she's paying. That boy is going to grow up with some sad misconceptions of the general female population and I am partly to blame. Oh well, all the power to him, I guess.

So here I'll end this expanse of drivel and prepare for my man to return home. He's taken to calling me Umaguma. I think it has something to do with good eating but I'm not really sure. See you, you ardvarchial specimen of an undiluted bile extraction from the inner core of the bowels of large and dirty birds. Remember me when you fly over and deposit.

Love, your fondest sister,<br>Rosanne

# Notes: Summer 84

She sounds a lot more settled and generally happier in this letter. She is applying for a better job at a hospital kitchen and is thinking long-term for her relationship. She even sounds more positive about her dear old friend Lydia and more supportive of her current friend Wanda. She seems happy for Wanda to have found a better apartment, even though, in previous letters, she sounded terribly frustrated by her nit-picking.

She is constantly making excuses for her boyfriend's behavior. Donny is too jealous to let her have any male friends but will get more comfortable with this idea as he gradually grows to trust her more. Unfortunately, that's not how this works in real life. A jealous, possessive man-baby will always be a jealous possessive man-baby. She can't see how he could ever move out west with her because of this issue. She has so many male friends back home so, apparently, he would lose his fucking mind in some kind of jealous rage.

She says that he needs all the attention. What a joke. How pathetic. Then she goes on with the fallacy that having babies will somehow improve this situation because he will have the attention he needs from his children. Wow. I think the children should need the attention from the father, not the other way around. I can't believe how delusional this is. She is secretly hoping he will change but unfortunately the die is already cast.

I'm somewhat ashamed to read the question of whether I will support her after she has kids because the honest answer was no. It was indeed our dear Mum who had to do it. I wasn't even around; I was living in Montreal. When I got back, Mum had already taken over the childcare through her postpartum depression, but I did spell her off occasionally. Rosanne was living in the basement at our parents' house and trying to put the pieces back together. Honestly, I was never a very good auntie because I had no interest in children at that time. I was young and selfish, completing my coursework at university and "sewing my wild oats". Of course, I cared about how Rosanne was doing and would visit her frequently, but beyond this, I wanted no part of any child-rearing.

I didn't know her friend Gord was interested in her romantically. I thought she only had eyes for his little brother Mack. It's good she has accepted that Mack has moved on with another woman. At least she has let go of that little fantasy and giant heartache. She sees his pattern of finding a sugar-mama to support him for what it is. She is slightly tempted by Gord's offer to head back home to Vancouver, but only fleetingly.

In every letter, I am struck by how Rosanne always talks about the decor of her apartment. It seems very important to her to make a nice home and decorate it tastefully. The simple things make her happy, like the tiny flowers on her bedspread or a couple of new dining chairs. I forgot she liked photography. She took a course in high school and obviously had a good eye. In fact, she was extremely creative and could have easily been a poet, an artisan, or an interior decorator, like our father.

# Summer 1984
## Visiting Her and Donny in Ottawa

I ARRIVED IN OTTAWA FOR AN ORIENTATION WITH WORLD UNIVERSITY Services on the way to Haiti. It was within walking distance of her place with Donny, who I had never met. They had been together for over a year, and she was extremely pregnant with her first child. I walked into her small, cluttered apartment to find Rosanne cooking and Donny lying on the couch watching baseball.

She came over and gave me a big hug and opened a beer for me. Then she introduced Donny.

"Hey, we finally meet! I've heard so much about you." I offered.

"Hey," he says without moving, "how's it going?"

"Good, Yah so congratulations on this baby that's obviously coming very soon right?"

"Yah, I hope it's a boy," he sounds unenthused, with a flat monotone voice.

Rosanne jumps in to save this lack-lustre conversation.

"So, I'm making us goulash eh, just like Mum's except I'm actually using some spices. Are you hungry?"

"You know me, I'm always hungry. So, I like your place. It seems really centrally located for getting around."

"Yah, I can walk to work in ten minutes or there's a bus stop right outside the building. It's pretty handy."

"But the landlady is a bitch," Don offers.

"She's not a bitch," Rosanne corrects him, "she gave me all that fabric to make those cushions and she gave me some dishes too."

"Yah, but she's always harping at me for wearing dirty work boots in the lobby. What am I supposed to do? Take my boots off outside the building? Fuck her."

"Isn't he delightful?" Rosanne says sarcastically. "Come on gorgeous, let's eat."

As we sit down, Don grabs a bottle of ketchup from the fridge and douses the goulash in red.

"Come on Don, you're ruining it! At least taste it first. It's delicious."

"To each their own. It's a free country last time I checked," he retorts.

Rosanne ignores him. "So, tell me about this trip to Haiti. Why the fuck are you going there anyhow?"

"I'm going because it's a free trip paid for by the World University Service of Canada and all I have to do is a research project on their education system and write an article about it at the end. I get to travel all over with twenty-five other students from across the country and it looks like a pretty fun group. We just met this morning for three hours to get the itinerary, do some bonding activities and we got yellow fever shots and malaria pills too. We are going to the Dominican Republic after Haiti too."

"Cool, well I hope there are some good-looking guys in your group. Maybe you'll fall in lerrrve," she exaggerates the word.

"Yah, I don't really care about that. I've still got Adam. He'll get back from tree planting around the same time that I get home."

"Is that still a thing?" she asks dubiously. "He's a little flaky though, wouldn't you say?"

"Yah, I guess he comes across that way at times. He just really thinks outside the box, that's all."

"Oh, is that what you're calling his particular brand of lunacy now?" she smiles.

Don jumps in. "Do you wanna go fishing this weekend? My Dad has a cottage on the Ottawa River, and we want to take you there on Saturday. "

"Well, I'm not much for fishing, but it sounds like a nice place to go. Can we swim in that river?"

"Yah, it's a little rocky but we can take the boat and find a spot if you want. We can stay overnight and come back Sunday. We'll have a barbeque and some beers. My brother and his family will be there too."

"Sounds great. Rosanne, is that comfortable for you in your current condition? Is there a bed for you?"

"Yah, it's fine. The mattress is pretty hard, but I can put some pillows underneath my belly. It is really nice there, even if Don's father is a dick."

"Fuck you. Don't talk about my dad that way," Don objects.

"Well, he is. He belittles you every chance he gets. He's never got your back. He treats you like shit."

"Mind your own goddamn business, Rosanne. As if your dad was any better. He sounds like a real prize."

Rosanne looks at me and smiles. "Well he has a point, eh?"

"Yah, I guess. Our Dad was pretty hard to live with, but he did support us in whatever we wanted to do at least."

"Yah, that's true," Rosanne admits. "Oh, the baby just moved. Do you want to feel it?" She grabs my hand and puts it on her belly.

"Holy crap, it's doing somersaults in there!"

Don looks proud," Yah, he's gonna be a strong little guy like his daddy."

"It might be a girl," Rosanne says, "but I doubt it. I've had a feeling all along that it's a boy."

"Have you picked out any names yet?" I ask.

"We like Michael for a boy and Fay for a girl," she says.

"He's getting my name for his middle name. No question," Don insists.

"Yes darling, you've made that abundantly clear," Rosanne says sarcastically. "We haven't figured out a girl's middle name yet, but I want Mum's name, obviously."

"I hate the name Joan," Don objects. "What about my grandma's name, Jean?"

"Yah, maybe," Rosanne considers. "We'll talk about it later. Let's go around the corner for some gelato. Mama needs ice-cream."

"I'm not coming," Don announces, "I'm watching the game."

"Fine, be that way," Rosanne says. "Come on sister."

We walk half a block and get a dish of gelato and sit down together.

"Isn't he just wonderful?" she asks sardonically.

"Um, no comment. Is he making any money to support you and the baby?"

"Sometimes, occasionally. Right now, he's got work for a week but it's only casual. He needs to find a permanent job but he's not very motivated. He likes to work for a short period and then collect EI (unemployment insurance) whenever he can. He's lazy as fuck."

"That's not great." I said. "Do you have enough for rent, food and diapers every month?"

"Barely. It's always a struggle, but somehow, we get by."

"Do you love him?" I ask.

"Yah, I really do. His bark is worse than his bite. He actually really loves me too, he's just not very good at expressing his emotions or showing affection. He's great in the sack though."

"Excellent," I am giving up at this point. "Well, I hope everything works out for you guys. God, you will be a mother in like a month. It's hard to fathom."

"I know, right? It's a frightening thought. Me, in charge of another living being. Who'd a thunk it?"

"Yah, it's a little scary, but you'll be a great mom. You have wanted a kid for so long."

"Well thanks for the vote of confidence Erwin. I really appreciate that eh?"

"Well, I gotta get going. I'm supposed to be back at the YWCA by 9:00. They have a curfew there."

"Ok sis, call me tomorrow. Love Yah." We hug it out.

"I love you too. See you tomorrow."

We drove down to Don's family cottage that weekend and Rosanne was smoking cigarettes and pot and drinking beer, despite my admonitions. We took their speed boat down the river to buy cheap beer and cigarettes from the First Nation across the bank in the USA. Don's family were friendly enough to us, but they were a motley crew. His brother seemed mean and condescending to him and his dad was a real hard ass.

On the second day, some argument ensued between Rosanne and Don, which resulted in Rosanne and I hitch-hiking back to Ottawa. Imagine a hugely pregnant woman hitch-hiking in the blazing heat of summer with a cigarette hanging out of her mouth and you pretty much get the picture. Needless to say, we got picked up quickly out of mercy.

When Don got back several hours later, he was in a foul mood. They argued some more, and Don smashed his hand through the kitchen table, breaking it in two, and then stormed out. Rosanne told me he was angry because she wouldn't let him sleep with me. I was shocked and told her this wasn't going to happen even if she had agreed to it. I realized in that moment that her relationship was doomed, and I felt very sorry for her. I needed to get out of there, so I went back to my room at the YWCA to cool off. She was mad at me for leaving and said on my way out the door, "Well, fuck you too!"

I walk back to my room at the YWCA wondering how this can possibly work out for her. This man is clearly a knuckle-dragging Cro-Magnon.

The next morning Rosanne called me to apologize, and we went out for breakfast and had a good long talk. I told how concerned I was that she was having a child with this asshole. She agreed that the situation was not ideal. We hugged and said our good-byes and I flew off to Haiti that afternoon.

# September 1984

## Card

Addressed to Sissy Spacecheck
(Ginger cat on the front)

Happy Belated 21st birthday

The cat signifies my lay-back attitude about birthdays in general this year. I missed not only you but Don and Wanda as well. I am sorry! Hope it was a success anyways and that you're not too depressed about being so old.

I haven't talked to you in a while eh. Was your trip (to Haiti) great and did you wow any exotic black men? What of the wonderful Adam? Don is much better and if all I'm told is true will continue this trend once the baby arrives. You'd love the new place, it's very homey and the cats would like it. We had a kitty visitor last night but I threw water out so we don't feel like adopting him. I've had plenty of visitors come and see the new place which I love. Hope you are as happy as I am now. Take good care of yourself and bust a little ass at the library this year eh! I wish you all you dream of, and for, dear. Look forward to hearing from you and seeing you at Xmas time.

Love and friendship always, Rosanne

# Overview: The Birth of Her First Child

AFTER MANY HOURS OF LABOUR, ROSANNE HAD A C-SECTION AND gave birth to a healthy baby boy. Unfortunately, her hormones took over at that point and she spiraled into a deep post-partum depression. Soon she had to fly home to our parents with the baby. Don was no use in any of this. My mother cared for that child for a year while Rosanne finally got the mood stabilizing and anti-depressant medications she so desperately needed. Eventually got her life back on track.

She decided to go back to college in pursuit of a better job. She enrolled in the psych nursing program, a two-year course, and worked the late shift at a local hotel bartending. She moved into her own apartment close to our parents and was doing well in school. Things were turning around.

She got hired immediately after graduating at the local forensic prison, where the worst mentally ill offenders in Canada are sent. She would work there successfully for many years. We were impressed by her mental toughness and ability to cope with probably one of the highest stress jobs on the planet. She rarely spoke of the clientele, probably due to some non-disclosure agreement, and she rarely complained about her duties. She was making good money for the first time in her life and things were looking up.

# October 1985

## (Vancouver to Montreal, where I'm doing some post-grad studies at McGill University)

Dear Evinrude 75 Horse McCusker,

I felt I should write since I meant to previous and did but never sent it. Mother says you were anxious and depressed about your courses but I would like to suggest that having to bathe and dump alone may be a major contributing factor to this moo (instead of mood). Perhaps if you were to feign an emergency once or twice with your roommates perhaps they too could be casually introduced to the joys of sharing a bathroom with others one knows quite little and enjoy it as much as you report to have done. See- your big sister, once again, solves a world crisis single handedly and comes out smiling like the idiot simpleton she is.

Loobis says hi too. I always thought Montreal was the last of hippie havens so was quite surprised to hear you say how trendy the women are. I guess most people are trendier than students and welfare moms so how are you to know?

I hope you settle in and are happy with everything out there. Wanda may be giving you a call soon as she sounds a little down about things and I think she would like to get away for a weekend (from Ottawa). I realize that you are busy but Wanda is very independent and would be content just to have a couch to crash on and a friendly face to greet her. She is pregnant again and has quit work right away to try to avoid having another miscarriage. Maybe you could give her a call or something at 555-555-5555. Sounds like she's not all keen to marry Ole, as he's quite a drinker and not everyone's idea of the perfect father. But then who is the perfect parent? Lots of people grew up ok with some perfectly shitty parents like some weirdos come from good homes too. Whatever.

I'm moving to a big one bedroom on Shaw Ave near the Cariboo pub. It's a corner suite so the living room is immense. It's on the ground floor so I won't have to lug stuff so much and there's a babysitter just down the hall with other kids and one of her own Michael's age to play with. Tom is going to move the big stuff for me and I guess the rest can go in Mom's, Brenda's and my car. I decided not to sell the car because I can insure it when my income tax comes and then even if I don't drive much it will be nice to have around. If I sold it I'd never get around to getting another one and I really like being mobile even if I can only make one journey a month.

Don the dog came over the other night and cried the blues about how he needs his family. I told him and am telling him that we won't make it but he's still here. I hope he goes to Alberta soon to work. I think he'll go there cause it's closer than Ontario and there is work available.

Jane got a job as the nurse in the prison at Grande Cache Alberta 2 hours from Jasper. Perfect for her, with nothing up there to spend money on except skiing. She was down for last week and I will miss having her around. We spent a day downtown at Granville Island and went to Robson and out by UBC for Greek food with Shari after. It was fun. I'm not speaking to Leah anymore and Wanda and Gord are moving to Edmonton at month's end so I'll be a little lost I guess.

Better get back to work. I'm going to go back to Douglas College and apply again for next year's Community Social Services Worker program too if they're still running it by then. It sure rains a lot here.

How can anyone expect to get work when you look like a drowned rat for the interviews!

Don's been doing some roofing on good days. I'm getting a summons sent out to him soon refusing him visiting 'til he takes a drug and alcohol program. He still says he's got no problem, but I believe that anyone who puts partying before food and shelter is fucked. We'll see what the judge has to say. Of course, all of this takes months so maybe he'll be off to work in Alberta by then. Anyways around here I guess I'll send this off before I get drooly. New address is { ...} same phone. Take it easy.

Love Rosanne and P. Lewis (another nickname for baby)

Drawing of a penguin standing on an ice floe beside a sign that says, "Absolutely no walruses."

# Notes: October 1985

In this letter from October 1985, you can hear the tail end phase of her postpartum depression talking. Her situation sounds pretty dismal at this point, but at least she had already moved out of our parents' house and was managing -more or less- on her own. The arrival of Don from Ontario was not a welcome surprise. He became a couch surfing burden to her for a time, even though there were plenty of welding jobs available. He never shared his little money with her or provided for his son. She did finally end up garnishing his wages through Family Court after he returned to Ontario.

I can hear that her mental health was improving when she talked about the goal of going back to school. It's a shame that this got bogged down in red tape and she felt so stymied. She was moving forward in the right direction. Keep in mind that the year prior to this she was a crying wreck living in our parents' basement, having returned from Ottawa with a newborn and severe postpartum depression. She could barely hold the baby without tears and now, a year on, this letter expresses much love and affection towards her son. She is doing much better.

# October 1985

## (Vanouver to Montreal)

Dear Iborin (Nirobi backwards) or Helmuteen McCusker (a name used in previous letter but mom lost it before it was mailed I think or maybe you did get it, in which case we'll have to think of something else.)

Dear threat of AIDS syndrome (hearty laughter somewhere off in the background (dad) moaning off to the left (mom),

In your letter, please explain this word "serious", it doesn't sound French or German; how is it that you are familiar with it and I am not? Would, do you think, it apply to missing the Jeffersons (on TV) to write you a letter? No, but I must say I'm a trifle concerned about Haitians and sex because I'm ignorant (almost) about like how you get AIDS and stuff. I understand the virus incubates for up to five years so I really super hope you don't like come down with this later eh. We know the high riskies and (would've thought we'd not sleep with them however "serious" they may be. (Thought I'd try it in context. How'd I do?)

Anyways around here it's too late so go ahead and enjoy your fun even if it is pale in comparison to some others, I don't know. God I am on a roll here so why stop now? You must stick out like a ruddy sore thumb against all the green and black background. Don't be a frog or especially a lily-pad on Halloween for Christ's sake. How's schoolwork? Racism in your part of the world?

Certainly misses you, does old P.Lewis and me. We're a long way off. Tings is ok wit us. We have a very nice bright new apartment with a living room big enough to play in and exercise and eat in all at once. I weigh 157 oh no and here I sit stuffing my face with taco chips and sour cream/ refried beans/ uncle Don's original southern recipe dip. Pigless, totally pigless.

Loobis is one now and he got your card but wonders what "fucked" means and if he can color his hair like that baby? Thanks eh. In future a strip-o-gram will do just fine. He got tons of presents and had a party of sorts on Saturday to celebrate. People dropped in all day and night; Cindy, Heather, Lydia, Debbie, Susan, Norma, Brenda and stuff. Heather hand-cartooned the most lubbly card for him and I framed it. He went to the petting zoo and out for lunch too.

Call Wanda eh. Invite her to Montreal for a weekend. She's preggie and needs a little break. Don still comes around but less frequently again, he's going to crack up soon. I think he's not quite right in the head at any rate. I've driven him there of course and all his problems are entirely my fault.

I plan to go to school in January. Not exactly sure what yet, police work or philosophy-English transfer programs at Douglas College are high on the maybe list-student loan city and inevitable years of poverty. I can't waitress anymore-I hate it. I worked one day at Tom's place at the mall and realized I was above that sort of thing. Just fuck it. Seriously! Anyhow I can't do anything else so it's either go to school or have more kids so I can stay on welfare. Kids grow up though and then I'll be 50 and have no skills or anything so I guess it's now or never.

Not much news otherwise I don't think. Know anyone who wants to buy a Torino? Only one dent and that's no shit. Money in the bank for now I guess. I fed Mikey spaghetti-o's for supper tonight. I reapplied at the hospital too. I guess I'd go back for the security if I got hired. We'll see. Mom and dad are fine except for dad's minor heart attack when you said you had a black man. We all love and miss you. The first year away is a toughy but hang in there kid.

Love from Rosanne and Mikey (who can walk, say duckie, quack, mama, bye-bye, popcorn, gran, oh-oh and stuff).

P.S. The Jeffersons was a re-run anyways around here.

# Notes: October 1985

IT'S INTERESTING TO READ HOW WE WERE THINKING ABOUT THE START of the AIDS crisis and felt unsure about everything. Haiti was said to be a hot-spot for the virus, so my having a relationship with a Haitian man was a hot topic of concern among the family. The relationship was short-lived and I had myself tested several times afterwards, but the fear was real and I realized later how stupid and careless I had been.

Rosanne's idea of having more children in order to stay on welfare seems amazingly idiotic except she was simply being practical about paying her bills, as many other single women have been in the past. I recall reading about the child propagation initiative in Quebec during the 50's and 60's organized by the Catholic church to try and populate the province with more French Catholics. Families were given money for each additional child, so this is not a new concept. The truth is, she really wanted a sibling for her son and loathed the idea of having an only child. I remember her saying at one point that she wanted to have ten boys. Perish the thought. She could barely cope with the two she ended up having.

Her mood sounds really positive and the idea of going back to school to make a better life sounded optimistic. There's also a big circle of women friends who came for Mikey's birthday party, so she's not feeling isolated anymore. She did end up going back to school and she did also get pregnant again by Don. She really wanted her kids to be full-blooded siblings, even though she knew Don was a lost cause at this point. It was setting the bar low, since she would never get any financial or emotional support from him. In fact, he moved back to Ontario and spent most of his life far away from his boys.

Rosanne soldiered on and completed her psych nursing program at college while also raising her two babies. She was tough and determined. Having our parents close by was a godsend in terms of babysitting and financial support, although they didn't have much extra money to give. Mom was an elementary school secretary. Dad sold furniture, carpets and draperies for a large department store and did interior design. We were a typical middle class suburban family who paid the bills every month. They couldn't afford for me to live in residence at university. I had to stay at home. Rosanne knew they would always help her in an emergency, but she was fiercely proud and wanted to be independent.

I admire her way of appreciating the little daily things of life: her son speaking a new word, the food they are enjoying, the tv show that's on, the kind gesture a friend made to draw a card. She wants me to reach out to her pregnant friend in Ottawa. Rosanne was always thoughtful of others and valued her friendships. Equally, she felt devastated when friendships ended, and I feel guilty now thinking about how our eventual rift must have felt like such a betrayal to her. She never forgave me for the separation. Even on my last visit to see her in the hospital, she was angry and crying and said I should "make things right". She still felt hurt and betrayed twenty years on, even though it was more about money and inheritances at this point. She wanted me to give her a big pile of money. The whole thing was just tragic.

# October 1985
## Vancouver to Montreal

Envelope addressed to NP Loobises

Dear Miss,

    The Grumps are both under the weather, so I haven't read your letter yet. Broccoli is a very important word and one should try most energetically to include it in a master's thesis about French literature if possible. Don't laugh-Mr. Broccoli (her baby son) is very sensitive and can't speak French very well so he gets his back up if you consider him green. His back is a lovely shade of thistle which he insists is not green at all but ocre (thistle he says is not a colour at all). Anyhow, he's terribly important so we'd better not say otherwise about it.

    I'm bored. It's Saturday night and it's month's end so I'm flat flippin' broke and Don's snoring in my bed and Michael is peaceful in his little room too. I really want to go to school in January but I can't send away my loan applications 'til or unless welfare asks for it and I can't see them 'til Nov.18th which is too late so I'm pissed off. I will not waitress so if I can't go to school I'm going to have a tantrum and tell them I'll bloody well get pregnant again and see how they like that. I'm beginning to think that ain't such a bad idea anyways. I can't get legal aid to get me a lawyer to go to court against Don because it's not urgent enough and generally the system makes me puke.

I'm quite content to stay at home with Michael. I have a nice place and once Don is in Alberta (soon) I don't care if I ever do anything again. I'll write articles or something and send them off to various publications so nobody can read them or anything. Maybe I'll just get high all the time- every day and start drinking really heavy. Ha ha. Never!

Jane sent me a birthday card from her prison in Grande Cache Alberta with $26.40 in it to put towards bus fare up there for a visit. I think it would be nice to get away a bit once Don's gone and on a day when I feel stable enough to take Mikey on a train or bus for 12-14 hours. I'll do just that I guess. The cost wouldn't be that bad and an adventure is always nice you know.

I'm going to buy myself a pair of badly needed shoes today, on special of course. I will get Xmas shopping on the weekend I hope if Don's UI in. He's four weeks behind, after changing address with them, so I've been putting up with him at great personal sacrifice for two weeks now but the extra money at the end will be great for Xmas. I hope I can get Michael a nice lot of stuff although Heather's girl must have something as she always gets my boy nice things. Jane too is asking for a fat present so Mom and Dad will get little stuff this year. Guess I'd better send yours off pronto or you'll not get it eh. Can't decide what for anyone but if mom or Don will watch the big P. I'm sure I can do it all at once no problem.

(End of letter I found I'd already written when I started the one on page two.)

Dear Miss N.

I am a shithead lately for writing a letter. If you're really going to get married, congratulations indeed. I am in awe of your guts. Even though I was always the apparent rebel of us I have always felt guilty inside about letting the Grumps down and as a result my self image has suffered and become almost self-defeating at times. Half the reason, at least, that I never married any of my suitors past is because whatever I do, even with Michael, I can ALWAYS hear mom's pleasant little voice in the back of my head giving the opposite advice to whatever I feel is ok at the time. This is no lie and it's my whole fuckupedness entire. I have only just realized this of late and I must say I admire, and envy somewhat, your ability to, in the crunch, do with an apparently clear conscience, what you know to be right for you. I lack the ultimate decisiveness you have. I listen too much, do too little, and analyze things out of all proportion rather than actually deciding anything at all. Do you know me to be this way? Of course you do. I can't say I like myself for it. I wish, I wish, I wish.

To change the subject, I think, I'm not certain yet, that Don is going back to Ontario soon. He has been here for two weeks now and is waiting for a couple of backed up UIC cheques with which he proposed to escape my sharp tongue. Once he's gone, I think I'll pay Jane a little visit in Grande Cache. To hell with Xmas gifts for anyone but you and Michael. I'm getting a portrait of Michael done for mom and dad and otherwise a little trinket should do. My finances are hopeless, I even went to the food bank last week. What a bunch of losers down there I tell yah. I didn't fit right in but I did get some free food. I got a new vacuum cleaner for $100 dollars at Woodward's. Dad and I went halves so at least we're clean if not affluent. It just sucks shit like crazy. Mrs. White (the neighbor who did vacuum demos) would be amazed. She gave Michael a lovely sweatshirt for his birthday. What a nice lady. Susan (did I tell you) got me a fig tree for a housewarming gift. How can I ever repay these kindnesses? What would life be without them?

I am going to bed; this letter is drippier and drippier and I'll cry or something if I keep it up. I'll get back to it tomorrow. No, I'll just mail it tomorrow. Kathy called the other day and got your address.

Naomi Lane

She said they'd gone through Tim's closet and had a bunch of stuff I could use for Michael. Very nice again. Guess I'll see her sometime soon. You'll get a letter too. We miss you and hope all is well and good and cheerful for you over there in the great white North.

Much love,<br>
Rosanne and Michael

# Notes: October 1985

THE FIRST PARAGRAPH OF THIS LETTER DRAWS ATTENTION TO HER BABY son's love of broccoli. I had just enrolled in the Master's in French Literature program (which I soon left for an honor's degree/ fifth year instead because I needed to become more fluent). I really enjoyed her word play here. It makes me smile.

It is apparent that Rosanne is up to her ears in bureaucratic red tape, between school, welfare, and Don's Unemployment Insurance claim. She is still supporting him financially. Her amazing solution to all of this is to tell everyone to go fuck themselves and get pregnant again with the same deadbeat that she desperately wants to get rid of. She's looking forward to him leaving for Alberta but at the same time, she wants his children.

She is generous to a fault. Even though she has no money, she is concerned about buying everyone gifts, even our parents and me. When a friend does her a good turn, she must reciprocate. She appreciates every little gesture of kindness. She naturally wants to buy gifts for her sons. I'm pleased that she is getting shoes for herself and not mentioning any gift for Don.

She longs for an escape and her good friend Jane, who worked as a prison guard, was so kind to send her bus fare, even though a twelve-hour bus ride with a baby sounds like absolute hell to me. It is clear that the impact of her ex-boyfriend Bob selling her car while she was in Ottawa has had a long-lasting impact on her life. She felt so tied down for at least two or three years because of his selfish move. She had to borrow Mum's car for every outing or ride the bus with a stroller.

Don came out west to see her and eventually wormed his way back into her bed. She naturally wants him to spend time with his son but he is as dysfunctional as ever.

The second half of the letter sounds more dire. She has given up on the idea of buying gifts because obviously Don's unemployment cheque never came through or, if it did, he didn't share any of it with her. Instead, she needs support from the Food Bank, which made me so angry at Don and also surprised she didn't go to our parents first. What a shitty Christmas.

She says she admires me for being decisive and ignoring our mother's constant advice. The truth is, I usually followed our mother's advice because it was mostly good advice. However, in this one instance, she was correct because I had fallen for a Haitian man and the parents definitely did not approve. It was the only time I stopped talking to Mum for a couple of months after I called her a racist hypocrite.

Rosanne says it was mother's little voice in her head that froze her in her tracks and prevented her from ever getting married. I can think of only one man she dated where a marriage could have worked and that was John the truck driver with the big family. She really seemed comfortable around his parents and siblings. He was also the only boyfriend she ever had who was a good earner. He was a little rough around the edges but generally treated her well. I don't recall our mother ever warning her not to marry but perhaps I wasn't privy to these conversations.

If Mum's critical voice really froze Rosanne in her tracks and gave her chronic self-doubt, that's a shame because Mum really just wanted what was best for her. However, she could be very judgemental and harsh at times. She would bluntly tell you to lose weight or that your ideas were idiotic. I remember waking up once at age twelve to retell my dream to her and Mum famously saying to me at the breakfast table," Nobody cares about your dreams." She had little imagination beyond getting things done efficiently and she hadn't a single romantic bone in her body, so anything to do with relationships was beyond her realm. She just couldn't relate to the emotional side of Rosanne or the turmoil of her relationships. Her advice never included this factor. It was just, "Shake it off and get on with it". Rosanne needed a softer touch.

# Late October 1985
## (Vancouver to Montreal)

(this letter paper is heavily soiled with brown coffee and banana stains)

Dear Mrs. Ella Loob in Murkwater,

Well ok. Fine. Sorry. I mean about the phone call. It wasn't so inspiring was it? Michael was very sorry not to have spoken to you but sends his love and wishes he could have a pillow fight with you instead. I was stoned so not as happy as I would like to have been. Anyways around here. Mom and dad came for supper last night and had some leftover clam sauce but I'm afraid I can't tell you what dad had for lunch yesterday. He frequently mentions Umbertino's across from the mall so I expect he'll try it out before too long.

I'm waiting to see if welfare will ok my return to education. I've an appointment on Nov.18th to discuss it. If I do go back I'm going to major in philosophy and hopefully get good enough grades to get into law school after. Big dreams but you never know I just might surprise everyone and make it.

As for Don, he's gone but will return before too long I'm sure. He really was trying in his own way to be good to me. He even started handing over more money at the end and bought me presents and stuff.

Seems like you've been gone a long time now. I have $1000 in the bank and when my next tax return comes in it'll be even more and I'm saving it all for a holiday for Michael and me. If Don's still in Ontario next summer when Wanda's had her baby and Ann gets wed I'll probably do a tour. Michael will be old enough to go and it will be a good break if I'm doing school.

Brenda says she'll take Michael for the last week in November 'til the Monday so I can go away a bit maybe to see Jane, although if I took the bus it would be a long trip to Alberta. Gotta go somewhere or I'll waste a perfect chance to get away. I wish I had friends closer than Alberta but if all else fails I'll go for a crazy weekend in Maple Ridge to see Carroll and stuff. Can't wait.

I got this little gift because I love you not because I owe you or expect anything in return. I know when I was away a present was even more better. Mom said that you owe her a few hundred for plane fare still and thinks you've forgotten. She's never ask for it but I think it would be nice if you can spare it to square that up.

Nice scribbly banana paper eh. Not to mention the fact that someone keeps stealing my pens. Just try to have a shandy! Grizzle grizzle choke on the shandy. Grizzle, someone eat a loobis (new word for milk snacks in a bottle). I feel like rushing out to Ontario to see Don. I know. But really I must love the guy even if it isn't good for me. Time will tell. If he really wants me he can send the fare. I bet if we both ended up out east, mom and dad would move out there too after Popcorn (the cat) dies.

Michael is so nice now. (Always was.) I think Don was a good dad, even if a rather poor husband. I always wondered when you were leaving why you never took Michael for a day or something but I guess he wouldn't remember you anyways by the time you get back this way. He forgets Don already and it's been less than a week.

I'm at least going to give this break 'til summer. Are you snowbound? Got a cozy fuck for those long winter nights? Wish I did! Brenda and Leah are the only people I see besides the grumps so I get

## Naomi Lane

a little weird sometimes. Mom and dad are weird. They exist in their own little world and I really don't fit in. Yes I do. Do- don't- do. When I get to school things will be way better I'm sure eh. Brenda and I are going to pub night at SFU real soon to meet hunks. Fat ones I guess. Tall ones for sure anyways. Well, I can't get witty for the life of me here so I guess I will go on and forget this letter ever existed.

Much love & friendly hugs and kisses<br>Rosanne and Michael

Roses are red
Violets are blue
If you believe that
You're a hemophiliac shrew.

# Notes: Late October 1985

THIS IS JUST BEFORE SHE STARTS COLLEGE AND BEFORE DON COMES back and gets her pregnant with her second son. She is starting to plan for the future, but she sounds lonely. She is counting only two friends who visit her regularly. She makes reference to the fact that if I stay in Montreal and she moves back to Ottawa to be with Don, our parents might follow. This is a total pipe dream because they never would. They loved Vancouver too much to move and both had steady jobs and a house.

It's surprising that she is still pining after Don, even though he's gone back east, but I understand how the father-son bond is a huge draw for all mothers. Giving that up is so hard. It was equally hard for me with my daughter going through divorce. Every time I saw a little girl running into her daddy's arms, I would fight the urge to cry. It dissipates over time, but single parenting was still brand new for Rosanne at this point.

It's nice to hear the fondness and affection for her one-year-old son in this letter. There were so many times where I saw her lose patience completely with him and yell obscenities at him, even as a toddler. It was hard to watch. She was like our father, impatient and hot-tempered. Much later in life, this would be diagnosed as a mood disorder and medicated. Too bad it didn't get properly diagnosed when the children were small. Perhaps she could have been a calmer mother and coped better with everything. As it was, she was very volatile. She smoked pot and a lot of cigarettes every day to self-medicate, but thankfully never became an alcoholic. She liked having a few drinks, but it never became a dependency.

    I think she also suffered from seasonal affective disorder, which made the depression worse in winter. Then again, who wouldn't find it hard to be stuck in a small apartment with a toddler in the rainy winter months in Vancouver? She was given anti-depressants after her post-partum crash, but I'm not sure if she was still on them during this time, as her situation had improved. Whatever the case, it never seemed like the medication was sufficient to balance her volatile mood swings and the children suffered for it. The switch would suddenly flip from happy and affectionate one minute to angry and verbally abusive or completely passive and withdrawn. The passive, withdrawn parent was often high.

# November 1985

## (Vancouver to Montreal)

Envelope addressed to Nairobi Percival Caradine

Dear Nam (alias boobless snibblenose wombatface charactereference vibration catastrophe),

He Yah. You called mom this morning eh. Must've gotten over your mad eh. Good cause she only wants the best for you eh. She mentioned to me, I assume so I'd mention to you, that your plane fare to Montreal is an outstanding debt of yours. Time to be independent in more ways than three I guess eh. That's the lecture. Did you enjoy it? Was it too wordy? Did I say too much? Think I'll get re-elected? Huh-do Yah-huh? Who cares what they want to hear as long as they keep paying. What am I talking about you ask? I don't know. Like I say, who cares?

I hear you also, after telling me on the phone, "No presents!" went and got my son something. Well I was thinking it was a bit early to mail things but here it goes and we probably won't meet Santa at all now the way the pigeons fly these days. Mr. Broccoli wants you. I want you. I need you. I can almost smell your breath. I'll bet you can even see your breath, in front of a fireplace, in complete darkness. Thick and heady stuff. Why go all the way to the cupboard for spices, meat tenderizers, oven cleaners, acne medicine, or mouthwash I always say.

I went to a party at Lydia's on the 15th for Randy's 30th birthday. She says I'm very negative and a put-down artist generally. Tell me it isn't so. She made me cry. I don't think she's too well if you ask me. All I said was that her dog, who lives outside, wanted a treat. I even had a genuine smile on my face at the time. Then, while we were chopping meat and cheese trays (not the trays, the meat and cheese) I asked her to do something she thought (in her infinite wisdom) that I might have done myself. All night she kept saying that I'd fit my pants much better if I got off my ass more often. I thought it was funny enough at the time but after everyone left and we were pretty gone she starts in on me. I had a cry thinking of all the times I was there for her at her convenience and she was never there for me. I didn't tell her that of course, I just refused to talk about it. She's hurt me for the last time. She doesn't want to know my son after all we've been through. Fuck her, she's jealous and has been going to the infertility thing at St. Paul's hospital. I hope she never has children because she's so selfish I think the kid would suffer for it.

Do you think I'm a bitter person? Of course you do.

Don's gone and it's starting to feel ok. I hope in a way he doesn't do what he says and come for Xmas. I like my life ok now and Michael is happy as usual. I go to find out about school one way or another tomorrow and I must say I have mixed feelings about it. So many different opinions have made it really hard on my limited decision making capacity. Oh well, we shall see eh. I admit I'm getting lazy and find myself quite content to piddle around most of the time and eat a lot. I of course think far too much about horse pies like "If you can do it so can I" and "I'll show mom and dad how wonderful I can be if I want to". I wish I liked myself a little better the way I am but then I'd probably have to give up being snide, smart-mouthed and impossible to cope with. I think I'm in an identity crisis or something.

I wonder if this will last long or drag on for an eternity. If the latter applies, I could give lectures.

    Heard any funny jokes lately or do you find Kathy's dad (also in Montreal) to be an interesting sort? Did she set up the meet with him or was it a chance encounter of the Loobis kind? Mercury hatchback city on wheels eh. Time I went to bed. I love you and I hope to see you soon.

Love Rosanne Celine Loobis

P.S. -Days later- School is all set- I'm going to take Phil. Eng. Psych. Sociology-really just a bag of reading but whatever. The previously referred to parcel was sent previous to this letter and the enclosed letter is quite old. I'll get pictures to you soon.

    I might be pregnant again! What do you think I should do about it if so? My IUD fell out last month and Donny accidentally came inside me, only partly, only once. How ironic that the first one took eight years and (if) this one only took $1/8$ of a second. Just my luck if so but I kinda feel like it's better to have two than just one and it may be my last chance to have un-step kids. Don't tell mom! Anyways I'll see Yah later. Love Yah.

Rosanne C. &<br>Mikey D.

# Notes: November 1985

THIS LETTER READS LIKE A RAMBLING STREAM OF CONSCIOUSNESS. Rosanne was very often high on pot, but this was not necessarily the case. This was how she thought and spoke all the time. She was a poet at heart, or the reader may see it more objectively as a mental health issue. I cannot be objective, as this free-wheeling form of expression was all I'd ever known from my sister.

There is a deep sadness here too. Her best friendship since high school is crumbling as Lydia insults her repeatedly and then calls her a negative put-down artist. Rosanne takes this very hard and starts to question her own self-worth. Never mind the fact that her best friend had recently married a heroin junkie after knowing him for a week. They were living in the boonies and, to be honest, Rosanne disapproved and was legitimately worried about her friend at this point. This must be the criticism that Lydia felt was rubbing her the wrong way. The two of them were equally wild and reckless. Apparently there had even been a threesome between them with Lydia's husband, so there must have been a lot more feelings underlying this feud than what we see here.

There is also tremendous ambivalence about going back to school. She expresses wanting to prove to me that if I can do it, she can do it too. She also wants to prove her capabilities to our parents, who valued education above all else. It's great to see, at the end of the letter, that she overcame her self-doubt and enrolled in a program. This would be the beginning of her psych nurse certification, which provided her a good income and benefits for the rest of her life.

Then we see the series of unfortunate events which became her second pregnancy. She and Don got back together for a short period of time because Rosanne admitted to me how she secretly wanted him to father a "full blooded sibling" for her son. She hated the idea of him being an only child. Magically, after the very first night they slept together, it happened. She was pregnant again.

Thankfully, she kicked Don out and went back to being a single mother. She had just become independent again. She had good female friends around her and our parents as support. I was traveling in Europe when I got the news that her second son was born. He was a very cute baby who got lots of attention from strangers and he was the apple of her eye. She was in a much better headspace this time around and had good maternity benefits from her job.

# Telephone conversation from Montreal

One day in Montreal, after I got home from my work as a cashier in a giant wholesale grocery store, the phone rang.

Rosanne announced, "Guess what? I'm pregnant again!"

"I just got your last letter. Donny is the father?"

"Yah, it's Donny. "

"Why did you sleep with him again? I thought you were done?"

"I am done with him, but I wanted Michael to have a real sibling, not a half-sibling."

"Jesus Christ Rosanne, where's your head at? You just got back on your feet with work and school. The timing is not great. Does Donny even know?"

"No, I haven't told him yet. I just found out and he's taking the Greyhound across Canada right now to go back home. I'll tell him when he gets settled. I don't want him running back here. I'm better off without him. He's fucking useless."

"Did you consider getting an abortion?"

"Yah, I considered it, but I never wanted an only child. That's a shitty life for any kid. I want Michael to have a sibling and I want them to be close in age so I'm having this baby."

I thought I had better say something supportive, since her mind seemed pretty made up already.

"Well, you can get Unemployment Insurance while you're off work so that should be enough to pay your bills and keep your apartment. Mum and Dad will help out too, but you know I'm going to Europe next summer, so I won't be around for your birth I'm afraid. "

"That's okay. I'm on medication now so I shouldn't get so fucked up emotionally after this one is born. I just hope I can stay in school, finish this program, and get a better job."

"Well, it should actually be easier to take courses while you're off on maternity leave," I said.

"Yah, probably, if I can ever get them to nap at the same time. Maybe after they go to bed at night I can study."

"So how many weeks along are you?"

"Just six. We only slept together once, I swear, and this happened. It's almost like it was meant to be."

"Well, I'm happy for you if you really wanted two kids. I wonder if it will be a boy or a girl."

"I plan on finding out as soon as I can. I want to decorate their room and get some cute girly things if it's a girl. I kind of hope it's a boy though because I already have everything for a boy so it would save me a lot of money on clothes and whatnot."

"Wow, I guess you haven't told Mum and Dad yet right?"

"No, I'm scared to. They're going to lose their fucking minds. After everything I went through with Michael, they are going to get mad and tell me I'm a fucking idiot."

"Yah probably, but who knows? They might surprise you and be excited about having another grandkid. They are both pretty fond of Michael after all."

"Yah, I guess so. I just know I'm going to get an earful about money and responsibilities and all that shit. They will think there's no way I can cope with another kid at this point, and they might be right. I can't predict how I'm going to be. I'm a little scared, to be honest."

"You'll be fine Rosanne. You've got a good doctor who understands you now and a cheap place to live. They can't fire you from your job for being pregnant. It's against the law. So, you can take whatever maternity time you need to get back on your feet afterwards. Even the coursework can wait if you need to take a break. Everything will work out, I promise."

"Thanks. I hope you're right.

"Okay but promise me you'll cut back on the cigarettes Rosanne."

"I'm trying. I'm only smoking like ten a day instead of a whole pack."

"And stop drinking beer too. Jeez Louise, you are a problem child," I said.

"You sound just like Mum, for fuck's sakes," she laughed.

"I know. I am just like Mum. I can't help it. But please take care of yourself better this time around.

"Okay kid, I promise."

# Late 1985

(A pink greeting card showing a man in a booth with two dump trucks passing by and a sign that reads: Fred's Dirt and Fill Dirt and Croissants)

Edwina,

How could anyone resist an opportunity like this one? Real western fill dirt and les croissants. A mouthful of each. Delight, pure and simple. When you throw up the result it's sod fit for building architectural splendors such as the world has never seen before. Flakey solid bits of true history. And for five cents extra you get extra butter and Fred will autograph your structure. There, I've gone on about it long enough.

Hope you are doing just fine and the boys are occupying your spare time for you. Leah and I are having suppers together Mondays and Wednesdays to help relieve the monotony here (or increase it as the case may be.) Don's gone to Ontario as you know. I had a big row with mom and dad about school the other day so I won't be going there so much anymore. They insist I should do a career program instead of a degree because "four years is a long time". Maybe when I was 18 it was, but now it's pretty short it seems. I'm not exactly looking forward to Xmas with just them and Michael. I won't have anyone to relate to. It's only one day. Anyways, I'm going to win $10,000 today so no problem. I'll just buy a condo and live happily ever after.

I really wish there was work here as I know that if work were plentiful I would be a lot more at ease with something to occupy my time. Michael is lovely but we get bored a lot. I'd sell my soul for a car. Waaah. Poor me. Never mind, it's all just talk. Write me sometime.

Love Rosanne<br>Bla bla bla

# Notes: Late 1985

IN THIS BRIEF LETTER, ROSANNE SOUNDS A LITTLE DEPRESSED OR perhaps simply bored. She's had a falling out with our parents about her college program, which they want to be job/trades oriented and shorter rather than leading into a degree. They probably see how housebound she is feeling and want her to get back to work sooner because she is happier working. They don't want to keep supporting her financially. They will eventually win out because she switched into the two-year psych nursing program and got a full-time job immediately afterwards. Christmas with the parents would have turned out fine because the grandson would have been the focus of everyone's attention and acted as a buffer.

It's good that she asked her friend Leah to have supper with her twice a week to break the routine and loneliness of being a single parent with no funds. This was a healthy proactive solution and I'm glad her friend came through for her.

It's also nice to see that she was not pining after Don, who had left to go back east. She seems to have made her peace with living without him in her life as a father figure for her son. This was another healthy choice at this point because he was like a stone around her neck. Having a child put Rosanne in the unusual circumstance of staying home and not being able to pick up men. She had never been single or celibate for this long since she lost her virginity at fourteen. It was no doubt sobering and extremely boring for her. I'm not sure if she ever did place a personal ad in the paper like she said she was considering. There were of course no cell phones or dating apps at this time.

She is self-aware enough to realize at the end of the letter that she is complaining a lot and feeling a bit sorry for herself. She had every right to whine, since she was living on welfare benefits, constantly broke and without a car. She felt completely trapped in her circumstances. So, what was her next best thing to do? Get pregnant again of course with the same useless asshole father. It was beyond belief for me and my parents that she thought having full-blooded siblings was the most important thing in her life at that point. It delayed getting out of the house and back into employment for another two years. It's honestly a miracle that she didn't spiral down into a depression after the second baby, but she fared much better. There was no postpartum depression this time around, thank god. I don't know if our mother could have picked up the pieces a second time because she and dad were getting into their sixties by then.

# February 1986

Dear Nyslobie Alefalter New Mexico Fatback Seabunkle Carnivor Raven Mathtutor Worstless Fuck (this letter is absolutely but not totally redundant so I'll post it along)

Hello, pleased to meet you; an honor in fact. I just want to brag. I got mom and dad to a photo studio and forced them to sit in front of a photographer and have their flicks taken. I pick up proofs tomorrow and if they're ok (even if they're hideous) I'm gonna buy us one each, a big one, sorta like hairblooms. See what you can do when you have children. What a ploy!

So I hear you have knee problems. Tut tut. Try geraniums red and delphiniums blue. I personally have a pregnancy related calcium deficiency affecting the muscles in my left buttock. Quite painful actually, although not to the extent that you and yours might imagine I suppose. Ooo I'm so snide. I go for an ultrasound on the demain to find out why my unsprung offspring is so extremely vast so soon. Twins?

I haven't heard from their father since he left, except last night he feebly attempted to call collect. Pussy. I'm doing ok, as in mediocre at school. Michael graduated to water babies II at swimming lessons and

I'm so proud of him. He is quite verbal now and is going to start his painting and playdough class in April.

Wanda and Ole bought a house and Willie (Nelson) and Emmy (-lou Harris) are coming to town together in March. I wanna go. Maybe Brenda'll go with me.

Is Whatsit alright in Haiti have you heard? Must worry you if not. How's school, work-men-roomates-etc? Life is extremely streamly quiet here- like I do diddly- school, swimming Saturday- mom and dad's Sunday- routine, boring and broke. It can only get better and at last there is a routine for the time being. So I'll say adieu, just wanted to say hi that's all.

Love Rosanne and Michael

# February 1986
## Part 2

Dear Marjorie Mainstream Caliber Upstart Whining Jane Unmarried Spinster (this letter is not also late but it will be quite redundant so I'm sending it along)

Hi again (not literally unfortunately),

So anyways around here. I guess you could say in a valid, logical, categorical, syllogism that: all people who are gainfully employed are jerks and all jerks have more money than I have, therefore all people who have more money than I have are gainfully employed. Jerks is the middle term, the gainfully employed is the minor and I, of course, am the major term. Think the teach'll like it? Do you? Like it?

Nice letter you wrote but I really think it's time you started taking "big craps" at more suitable moments. It's not that I mind, I just hope you don't do this sort of thing to all the people you write to, i.e. Dear Dean of Admissions, oh excuse me....etc. You see it could develop into a really bad habit.

Speaking of bad habits, as well as big craps, I've been invited to Miss Lydia's wedding, again. Haven't spoken to her in months and she sends it through the mail, so I think I'll ever so politely decline, and perhaps even excuse myself, mid-reply, for a large and noisy crap.

She's holding it at Ruskin for the convenience of all her friends and rellies too so like forget it eh. Later.

It's hard to avoid I see. I too have just gone and taken a "nice crap". I feel so hypocritical. My belly isn't so terribly big yet but will be soon. My ultrasound says I'm three weeks further along than we thought so June 30th June 30th (a title of a Richard Brautigan book of stupid poems) is now the date of arrival of planet neuclon. It waved at me too. Hi mom (and dad) that makes me mad doesn't it? C'est la vie. Anyways around here.

School is ok sometimes. My Children's Lit. prof is really excruciatingly boring me to death but at least the homework is minuscule. Criminal psychology is enthralling. I could listen to that shit all day and still want more, and Logic is well, you know. Glad to hear you're doing so well. I don't think I'm going to push myself to great grades but we'll see. Donny is a bonafide psychopath and will grow out of it before he's 40. Good for him if the booze doesn't kill him first in one way or another. Anyways, I don't care, not around here, and not around there.

Well, there you have it, my life in a nutshell. If only my body would go into one. I have a lovely profile of your nose on file from the pics I took and the vastly expensive photos of ma and pa and P. (nickname for Michael). Photos are due in about the end of March. You may have to frame yours yourself and since dad "helped" me choose them you are getting a slightly smaller one than me but more variety. It was a nightmare trying to help Mikey but the photo lady understood what was going on during this proofs session. Dad, of course, was the problem and his hearing aid was not. Period. I think sometimes that, had I stayed in Ottawa, I would have gotten over the "bad spell" just the same and maybe I would have been well off out of their hair. Dreams, it's all a dream.

It's snack time for all the preggies now, and then off to bed like all good unlittle people.

Tata (or gaga, as they say in English)<br>Batman signing off to Ms. All of the Above

Generally.

(inside a big heart drawing) A very happy, if somewhat belated, Valentine's day to you as well as a portrait of what the picture might have looked like had you not been so excruciatingly stubborn about not letting me take a picture of your posterior on that fated day. It could also be a balloon or my breasts or my belly, something.

(drawing of a Canadian nickel) It's not enough is it? Jerk!

# Notes: February 1986

It's lovely to hear how proud she was of Michael as a toddler and how she had him enrolled in various creative activities. I never got to hear much of these positive parenting moments so it's very endearing.

When she says that Donny will grow out of being a psychopath by the time he's 40, that is her making a joke because I very much doubt that he was clever enough to say this himself.

It's interesting to hear how much she enjoys criminal psychology. She says she could listen to that shit all day. This is the field she ended up working in, of course, which was obviously a good choice since it fascinated her. In fact, this fascination probably influenced every choice of boyfriend she ever made.

Her logic assignment about the gainfully employed is very clever and also very personally meaningful to her. She had a huge distrust of anyone wealthy or even remotely well off. That's why she was repeatedly dated men who had no money. (The one exception was Dominic in Ottawa, who she used as a means to an end.) She saw herself as blue collar and one of the people. In reality she wore this as a badge of honor and didn't really want to move up in the world to a place where she might be treated with disdain by the working poor.

*Letters From My Dead Sister*

She is mad at her friend Lydia so it's tongue in cheek when she says the wedding is in Ruskin for the convenience of all her friends and relatives because Ruskin is way outside of Vancouver in "the sticks". She is saying that it's another selfish move on Lydia's part.

The reference to Dad being the problem during the photoshoot is no doubt accurate. He was hard of hearing but much more than that, he was generally difficult. Every time we went out in public he was embarrassing. He would speak loudly to people in an antiquated condescending manner or engage waitresses in long conversations when they were extremely busy. In short, he would always make a scene and be too long winded. We were always cringing and apologizing for his behavior.

It sounds delusional at the end of the letter, when she says that maybe if she had just stayed in Ottawa, she would have gotten over the "bad spell", meaning the year of postpartum depression, but then she quickly realizes this is all but a dream. She hates being so reliant on our parents. She loves them dearly, but they are clearly driving her crazy and she understandably wants to be financially independent.

# June 1986

(A card which reads "Have a wonderful time and bring home lots of happy memories" because I'm on my way to Europe. She is 8 months pregnant with her second child.)

>Dear Travela Mermaid Sparrowhawk Up & Down Roller Coaster Albatross Black /Market Sinister Pig,
>    The latter referring primarily to any person found in the company of one Kermit the Frog, and specifically, of course, to yourself there. No is the monosyllabic answer to all the above questions; specifically, of course, the one about Edward. His name is actually Fay Rhea or FR for short. This having consistently nothing to do with the frog but a great deal to do with the similarly unnamed species of the species. In short, pilfering, insufferable, nurselike, anti-lubricants of the sloth swathed arseholes of camels.
>    To be brief, I'm having a Coors. We are having a Coors (her and her unborn baby). You vastly underestimate Exhibit B2 (meaning her stomach). Large is not a big enough word and (as one pinhead to another) I find your profile stunning. Wanda had a female exhibit on

April 26th, that ill fated day when all of Europe and those traveling abroad (this kills me) were threatened by the carcinogens of nuclear fallout that is filtering its way at this very moment out from behind the iron (told them lead) curtain. Do you realize that you have called home (Edward Trafalgar) 936 times in the past two months, each time with a totally awesome nit of news. 60 Minutes is looking for you, Mr. Rogers was actually seen to perspire and Mr. Reagan had a nap upon hearing it all. I, on the other hand, and much to Mr. Roger's dismay, took a Coors over to the Honkers Place (Sesame Street) and prayed for rain. Bad sentence structure indeed.

My Lit. prof was humongously concerned over my overt wordiness and honored my exquisite literary presence with a C+, not knowing of course that I would have given her a similar hunk of piss. A B in Crim. was ok. That was a good course and I feel in love (imperfectly) with my prof. I'm sure he felt the same.

Let's start saving these letters, along with any previously uneaten cheese bagels, and present them as a doctoral thesis in pygmalion. K?

What a stunned time to go to the far side of the pond. You will surely miss the exposition (EXPO 86) and the opening of the new Lougheed Mall (our local shopping centre). Up to you of course, again, but... Mebeba or Mebebodda is words referring to "Make me a ball of playdough" or "I want a bottle of milk" respectively and mama is pronounced exactly the way Auntie Tilly said it was. Boddas do not contain anything but milk at all, ever, and we prefer about 75 Mebebos an hour on a regular production schedule. The management is having a tantrum at the moment because my rabbit is not being drawn immediately again. Life is so imperfect. Anyways here are some courses that I'm sure are available anywhere (particularly Copenhagen (where I'm going) that you might like to take:

Don't Worry about Fallout

The World is a Wonderful Place

Venus here is Not so Great

Bon Voyage, Rosanne and Michael

# Notes : June 1986

THIS LETTER IS A CLASSIC EXAMPLE OF THE RAMBLING POET'S MIND OF my sister. I don't even think most people would find it intelligible, but I understand every innuendo. She explains much of what is happening from her son's perspective in toddler language. Her second baby is due in a month and her belly is huge. She is going to name it Fay Rhea if it's a girl, who would then have the same initials as our father, Franz Robert. She's still drinking beer, which she's always proud to tell me because she's flouting societal norms of behavior.

She references Chernobyl and wonders why I am traveling to Europe after this disaster, thereby exposing myself to nuclear fallout. What she doesn't reference is Mad Cow Disease, which was rampant in England in 1986. Just my visiting there would prevent me from donating blood for years. I would travel for three months that summer, also working in England as a temp for a large car rental firm, which was quite fun and gave me a real glimpse into daily English life. I did go on to Paris, Amsterdam, Copenhagen and Florence and stayed mostly for free with relatives or friends of friends.

While I was at our aunt and uncle's place in England, I woke up one morning in July just knowing with all my being that Rosanne had given birth and soon thereafter came the phone call from our parents.

There would be no Fay Wray, for it was another son she would call Neil. She had a C-section again and both mom and baby were healthy and doing fine.

This put her schooling on hold, of course, for another year. We were all so relieved that she did not spiral into a deep postpartum depression after this baby came. In fact, she was quite besotted with him, probably because he looked exactly like her, and she called him an "easy baby".

She was able to finish her schooling, which was most impressive, given her circumstances. After a year of ridiculous back-and-forth with Donny where he would show up occasionally and spend time with his boys, Rosanne finally got him out of her life for good. She convinced him to stay with his own family in Ontario and leave her alone. She was much better off without him because he was a complete loser. She received a pittance of child support from his wages. This, of course, only drove him to work less and collect more government benefits.

# July 1986
## Vancouver to England

Dear Naomi,

    Seriously, you know the dreams joke-nothing quite so interesting (or redundant) as other people's dreams (our mother always said). Excepting one item-having your mom stay with you for two whole weeks. I really really appreciate having her and we have good laughs and a drink and Miami Vice together, but you know how it can be. I quit smoking for two whole weeks but the second week I got so bitchy with poor Michael, who has gone through so much already with moving and me being in the hospital and now Neil, that I've taken it up again I'm afraid. When they're older and can understand why I'm a bag I'll try again. I feel gutless but better.

    Neil is an easy baby who sleeps a lot and makes very little noise so that's great and I recovered really fast from the surgery so all's much better than expected all round. The move was a disaster, did you hear? I couldn't move into my place the day I booked the movers, for it wasn't ready. I had to store my stuff in a vacant townhouse for almost a week 'til the morning I was going into hospital. I ended up just leaving everything for poor mom to sort out, which didn't get completely done of course so I came home and got busy right away. She did an awful lot though and had that Michael to deal with as well.

Dad was a gem- if it weren't for him and GVRD contacts I'd be out on the street for that week. He had the lady in the rental office shitting that she'd be unemployed if I didn't get somewhere to stay and someone to move my stuff from one place to this one. It worked. Nice place here- you should come see it.

So, you are a bit of a laugh in my eyes only as of late. First you make and receive numerous long-distance calls seeking and consuming advice and then I get this letter with such a vile accusation in it-mostly it seems to me like about things you done to yo sef man. I agree perhaps on the mail issue, but honestly "Dad, what should I do now?" You knew he wouldn't see things your way or you should have. I'm on the outside and I say clean your ears next time you're in de wata.

I miss you and I'm saving all our letters so we can make our own Bloom County comic strip when you come home and make a fortune. Instead of Berke Breathed, we'll be Someone Farted (or just initial F.) loudly eh? Ok you come up with a better one then. Just see if you can. Betcha $10 you can't. Dream on! Suck a fattie. Can't use fattie-it's my word. I know your word-it's Edward, isn't it?-redundant. Anyway, say hi to Liz and Chuck and Di for me if they're around.

Love and kisses and two half eaten banana cake slices with rancid butter on them,
Rosanne, Michael and Neil

# Notes : July 1986

- *Berke Breathed was a popular newspaper comic at this time.
- * Edward was one of her nicknames for me, or alternatively, Edwin, Edwina.
- *Liz refers to Queen Elizabeth

THIS LETTER ILLUSTRATES JUST HOW MUCH OUR PARENTS CAME through for her when the chips were down. She had to move and give birth at the same time, which is clearly impossible, so they stepped up and did everything. I didn't know Dad had pulled some strings with his business contacts to get her an empty apartment to store her furniture. I didn't even know he had these kinds of contacts. And Mum was clearly a champion to look after her two-year-old son while cleaning and setting up her new apartment. I was in Europe and oblivious to any of these goings-on.

She tried to quit smoking about a million times, but it never lasted long. She was a true addict, and she was fully aware of how her mood changed with the withdrawal. I can see how Mum staying with her for two weeks postpartum would drive her to start smoking again but she was lucky to have the support while her C-section healed. Mum was a saint, chasing after Michael while Rosanne rested and tended to her newborn. We really did have wonderful caring parents. Even though Rosanne bucked their authority all through her teenage years, she knew they were there for her during the difficult times.

When she says I am a bit of a laugh in her eyes, she is putting me in my place about some communication with Dad. I was traveling through Europe, and he wanted me to visit his birth city of Frankfurt, spend time with our remaining cousins there, and see his two family homes that were taken by the Nazis. I ignored his request, and he was upset with me. Rosanne was good at putting me in my place when I was in the wrong, as I knew I was in this instance. I didn't realize how upset he was until I got home and then I deeply regretted not going. I made up for it on a later trip, but he had already died by then.

# July 1986

## (I'm back in Montreal)

Envelope addressed to Naomi Classic

My Dearest Edward,

So nice to receive your long-awaited correspondence! My sixth sense told me, long ago, that there would be no presence or presents from you, Ed, this season. So I went out and blew all my bucks on the kids. Michael mostly. He is getting heaps of stuff from me and assorted other admirers. Neil gets a little but-Neil is a little bit.

We are going to the White's house this year for Xmas dinner because I say so. Mom said no, but while I was talking to Betty to thank her for the Hawaiian shell night-light and then to Robert about Michael, who had his knees stuck fast through the rungs of his crib at the time, I said yes. It's more funner even if mom doesn't think so. She's going. Michael pulled himself out, (I didn't force them out cause I didn't want to break his knees), just before Mr. White left to come to the rescue so that was ok. Susan and I went out to see Three Amigos last night and went for drinks. She's going to Whistler on the 17th to ski, work, live with Adam 'til summer, then either three semesters in a row or China or something. She'll write you a Xmas letter she says.

I'm doing aerobics thrice weekly now and it's not bad. I may look for work in March but I'm not sure yet. I have to consult my social worker to see if it's worth it. I started proceedings to hound Don for money through the social worker last week against my better judgement. I don't want him here with access to these boys, I'd rather be broke. I sort of have a hunch that January will be an interesting month. Don says he's coming, even though I said no, and John the Eskimo says he may also pay a visit. Soap city, I hope not.

Things are going so smoothly now. I was hoping to move into Tom's house now that he bought one in Delta but his sister Christine got it. I tried to get to Cap (the landlord) first but Tom put in a good word for her. I am furious about it because when Brenda left her place, he talked me out of that one and I told him I wanted his house. I will speak to Brenda I guess (I don't feel great towards her now either) but never to Tom or any of his blood again. Christine needs that place like she needs a new ass or something. Fuck em. Delta isn't far enough away.

Neil says Ahhhh (hi ho). Lydia is making my ring at last with a black pearl-yay! I'm going to a party at Norma's on the 20th to remind her of it. What else is new? AIDS. Heard about it? Ask those Haitians to test pure first because this disease is fatal.

I was thinking of answering personal ads or placing one myself. I mean I never SEE a guy let alone fuck one. It's been a celibate year and Rosie (herself) is a tired old gal (Miss Palm as the fellows call her). I just feel overwhelmingly great about '87 tho' I think. Or as much as one can handle with the two rugrats around. Pitter patter, pitter patter.

Well dad's picking us up to go see the doc so I'll pick this up and finish it later. (I never fart or shit so I can't relate that to you.) You will think back upon the discussion of such matter with those members of the opposite sex and blush in years to come. Trust me, I know they're Jewish, but still.

Anyways or otherwise, Michael the Eloquent will discuss these things at length with you presently. He assures me that he's not lovely; he's Michael. He knows about these things almost better than I do. He is certainly a Macdermittish (father's surname) little persona, but I have him, nonetheless. Broccoli is redundant, but breakfast is nice and a little lithpe (lisp) helps all words become, shall I say, groth. "I don't like it, thith Neil crying mom," and so on. Or a little grin, "I thmack Neil and Neil crying mom," and so on. Charming. Obviously things like news are running out here. As I mentioned, I don't fart or shit so-

Hope your Christmas was good<br>
Guess we'll phone eh,<br>
Happy '87<br>
Love Rosanne-loo<br>
Mikey-D.and<br>
Neil-B.

# Notes: July 1986

ROSANNE SOUNDS SO MUCH BETTER IN THIS LETTER. SHE IS OPTIMISTIC about the future and making plans. She has started exercising regularly and is considering going back to work. She has followed up on garnisheeing Don's wages for child support and her affection for her kids really shines through. She sounds like a proud, loving mother. She has even taken the initiative of organizing Xmas dinner with our parents' friendly and generous neighbors. She is looking forward to getting laid and considering putting out a personal ad to meet someone new. All these are positive steps towards happiness. She signs off by saying that '87 will be a much better year.

She said Johnny the Eskimo might visit soon. He was another short dark stocky guy from way up North who she met god knows where. He came for an awkward dinner at our family home where he spoke not one word.

It's a shame her best friends, Tom and Brenda, screwed her over in the house rental arrangement. The two rental houses were side by side; Rosanne and Brenda lived in one and Tom lived next door. When Rosanne moved to Ottawa, Tom and Brenda got together and became a couple, moving into one house. When Rosanne came back, they didn't offer her the second house, even though she had asked for it. Instead, they gave it to Tom's sister Christine. Rosanne was very hurt by this, and you can hear her anger and resentment. She eventually cut ties with Brenda, which was a tremendous loss, since Brenda had been one of her most supportive friends for years.

She was still very concerned about me having a Haitian boyfriend in Montreal because of the AIDS crisis. It was a scary time, and nobody knew what was going on. Everyone thought, at first, that it was a disease only gay men could contract, but that proved false of course. Then there was no cure in sight and people were dying in droves. I did get myself tested multiple times after the brief relationship ended and was so relieved to come away unscathed. It was touching to hear how much she cared about my wellbeing at the time.

I was a shit for not sending Xmas gifts for the boys, but I was also a broke student living off student loans and she understood that and gave me a pass. I was also very sure my parents were providing the necessary supplies she needed as well as some extra toys. Our parents were solid as a rock, as you can see by our dad picking her up for the doctor's appointment.

My mother took the boys frequently to help her out, even though she worked full time and was sixty at this point. She was a saint in my opinion, but I am biased of course. She would also let us use her car for job interviews and such. She took the bus to work for three months in 1987 while I was doing my teaching practicum on the other side of the city so I could use her car. I look back on this sacrifice now with tremendous gratitude.

In 1987 I moved back home from Montreal to do my teaching qualification year at university. I got hired immediately afterwards and started full-time, got my first car, met and moved in with my soon to be first husband. Things were still really good between Rosanne and I during this period.

# August 1986
## England

Dear N'oublie pas ???

And that was it. No opening remarks whatsoever. Neil went to bed at 7:30-can you dig that? Michael is calling every Eugene, Dominic and Harry "my daddy"- can you dig that? It's, or was, your birthday-did you dig that? At least she resorts to proper punctuation- at the age of 28- can you dig that-eh?

The Peruvian flautist played Bridge Over Troubled Water for me and dad at Expo and I saw Peter Ramsey and he looks just like Jack Ramsey-wild- who would've guessed? Brenda's pregnant-Tom's excited-they're living at his house and getting wed.

Don got hung up on and cursed last time I heard of him. Daddy indeed! Happy birthday Namsie. Susan is moving home. Never saw Kathy. I like beer and potato crisps. I managed to con more daycare for Michael even tho' I'm not doing anything, he likes it so much. Mom and dad are tedious to a point- I see too much of them and too little of anyone else. Very good to me-drive me all over hell's half acre and back. Mom's spent a record 4.5 million on her car this year. Nimrods those people when it comes to car maintenance, I'm afraid. We all have flaws. We do not, however, all have cars. Pooh.

## Naomi Lane

I'm great- two under two and I even got a little colour this summer and I only weigh (the bi-word being only) 170 lbs. Ah well, at least I have hair. I sort of pick up that you are sorry about the aforementioned hair (dyed blond) but it looks cute, but requires a little more makeup or feminine attire I think.

Perhaps at Uncle Paul's (photo included) you weren't up to snuff or it's a bad picture. "In the garden one, you look so much nicer Naomi." I miss your face kid. Sorry, did that make you sad? I'd be there if I had the pluck. You bet. No plucks here- no bucks and no plucks. Ain't nobody here but us chickens anyways around here. Buy a watch? Boy, once you get on that Schreiber drift (her Jewish voice). It starts slow but once you get going-jeez. That's sort of Catcher in the Ryeish anyways. Very very interesting eh. I see you bought yourself a new sweater/ blazer/ jacket thing. I want it. You can even send it COD if you want. It looks nice on you-so anyways.

Happy Birthday  
Love from all of us  
Rosanne, Michael and Neil

# Notes: August 1986

Rosanne convinced me to dye my hair blond when I was twenty-three. I remember sitting in her room in the basement listening to music when she said,

"You have such pretty blue eyes. Why don't we dye your hair blond? It would make your eyes pop. That mousy-brown hair makes you invisible."

Was that a back-handed compliment? Perhaps, but from her I took it as gospel. So we went to the drug store to buy the kit. She applied it to my wet hair and we waited in the kitchen while she smoked and told me about her date with a married man named Graham who she met at the bar where she worked. Graham was a used car dealer so she thought he could get her a deal if she just kept on sleeping with him for a little while. They would meet at a local hotel for a few hours and then he had to go back to his wife and kids. Unfortunately, the car never materialized, and it fizzled out. She said he was bad in bed.

After forty minutes, she rinsed the dye out for me in the kitchen sink. After blow drying, she complimented me and said it looked way better. I was thrilled with the transformation and people have always told me they are shocked to learn it isn't my natural color. I have been blond for all of my thirty-five years since.

When she says in the letter that she "has no pluck", she is reflecting on her fear of traveling. Even before she had children, she never ventured far from the nest. This always struck me as odd. I would have thought she was much more outgoing than I was, but as we got older, I realized that the opposite was true. I traveled a lot on my own and had way more confidence about staying with relatives and / or even total strangers. Friends of friends would hook me up with free accommodation all over Europe. I embraced every new city with my circle of friends and acquaintances getting ever wider. Rosanne became a real homebody and kept the same small group of friends for many years.

It was shocking to me that she had any fears at all. I had always pictured her as the adventurous one. In truth, she mostly just wanted children. She wanted to create a traditional nest and be loved unconditionally. She always spoke of having children she could party with. This was part of the dream of having her children become her best friends, who would never abandon her like her girlfriends and boyfriends had. She very rarely spoke of wanting a wedding to any man. I can only think of two boyfriends where she envisioned this happening. Her expectations of all the men she dated were abysmally low. It's like she always knew that relationships would eventually end in disappointment. She had learned not to trust the men she was with and somehow, she always picked the wrong guy. Her world stayed small because there was never any money to dream big. It was like a self-fulfilling prophecy.

# October 1986

Envelope addressed to Miss N. Shepherd from Miss R. Cowbrand

Dearest Nirobeli Dobeli Boo,

Yoohoo. U2. Hullabaloo. Rooty Tooty Mr. Magoo. Honey Bun Loo. How are you? And a howdy doo? Boo! Happy Halloween eh. What are you going to be? A carefully preserved-in-ice-Saskatchewan-peace-missionary-come-hippy? Me too. No way, surely. You could be better off than you are- you could be swinging on a star. And all the monkeys aren't in the zoo-every day you meet quite a few. Deep city Atlantis eh. One could always opt for the 10 day workshop in creative exorcism or financial wizardry or combine the two like I did and do financial exorcism. "Money be gone!" I shout and so be it. Make me an offer I can't refuse. Sidewinder is a nice word today. Totally meaningless but. Grain storage is another spacious accommodation for pesky rodents such as do accumulate therein also.

Life is pretty quiet in general and I do squat. Michael says "Do my name" and "No" a lot. He has Auntie Nammy confused with Beryl /

Mrs. Readman. These are all the same person to him. Your picture is being used as an Auntie Nammy flashcard henceforth to dispel such myth. Be cool, it's ok. Neil is fairly nonplussed about the Auntie Nammy situation to date but is keenly interested in bowel movements or shits.

I left you here for days and you didn't even know it did you? I went off and wrote all my reasonable, serious, dutiful letters and then came back here and am currently relating to you my innermost tragedies, comedies and to wit???? Not only that but now I'm going to bed.

We have replaced the name (for her eldest) Mr. Broccoli (accent on the Bro) with just plain Peanut and Neil is the Smiling Schlemiel. Like it? Luis Gomez and wife and kids moved into this building. He's going back to Venezuela next month and she is staying 'til June. I hope we see plenty of them. Nice kids- nice family actually. Luis has a good heart and I can forgive his conceit since he is very brazen about it. My friend Elspeth is moving in here too. This feces-*waste of human genre-kak-pooh-surplus cheesecake-black pudding and bananas-is a slight problem for me as she makes herself scarce 123456789 not scarce all the fucking time. I must be tough-I must be strong-" Go away" I must say- to Don the daddy also. He wants back and Michael will say "I see my daddy!" and stuff. If I had a guy I wouldn't even consider it but it will literally be years before I ever meet anyone at the rate I'm going. I really want sex badly at this point and I'm terrified I'll weaken and go for it for bad reasons. Pray for me. I'm getting my tubes tied on Nov.3-ringed-not tied. It's reversible in a pinch so on the off chance that I ever recover from this stage of my life and ever want to do it again I maybe can.

Mama is now trying to convince me to wait until she retires to go back to work. Michael can go to the school by her place. Sure, I'll just sit in this apartment for three years, no problem. Then she'll decide to move to New Mexico or something else. Uh-uh (no). Instead of taking downers I am now taking mega B stress formula vitamins with C and iron. Yeah what a buzz-good for one's skin Mrs. White tells me.

Let's see what else is new? Michael is a bird herder at heart and can rustle ducks, crows, robins, pigeons and what have you better than anyone. My hair is root city-Kunta Kinte plus man. I think I'll grow my bangs out since I'm halfway there and no one's looking anyways. Go back to my natural color (auburn) more or less too. No haircuts for me yet. Wow eh. Astounding news suitable for Loser Weekly or Born Dumb. Abstinence sucks-all the rest fucks. Wowee even.

Ok this time I am going to bed- later. On third thought I might as well mail this tomorrow with the rest. I'm talking to mom on the phone here for your address and she's reading an article on absent-minded people (a funny poem) and telling of all the garden and Moody's walk and dial-a-dietician-what a gal. Nice pigout tea at school too. In the not so background Dad tries to listen to the news at volume 35.000.000 decibels and can't hear it very well. Life goes on after Expo is what he wants to hear.

I love you,<br>Rosanne

# Notes: October 1986

THIS MAY BE HER MOST UNHINGED LETTER YET. SHE IS RAMBLING LIKE she is high, but this is just her stream-of-consciousness style of writing. She is outwardly expressing her inner dialogue as well as her silly baby language with her boys. She constantly makes up new words. I am so used to this that it doesn't even strike me as odd, but I'm guessing it's pretty darn strange for every other reader. It does sound like spending all her time trapped in a small apartment with a toddler and a newborn is starting to take its toll on her mental health though.

It's sweet that she is using my photo to teach her son who I am in the family, since I am in Montreal. She has also made friends with a Venezuelan family in her building, which is healthy. She seems nonplussed that her friend Elspeth has moved into the complex as well and somehow wants to avoid her. Don has come back from Alberta or Ontario, where he was working, and she is afraid of her own weakness. She desperately wants sex but knows that letting him back into her life and bed would be a big mistake. It's hard to say no to your kids' father when they ask for their daddy. At least she is getting her tubes tied so she cannot get pregnant by him a third time.

It's good to hear that she has traded "downers" for vitamins. I'm not sure which downers she was taking but I'm sure it wasn't a great option for a depressive person. Our mother's offer to do her childcare after she retires is an amazingly kind gesture, in my opinion. Rosanne is understandably not willing to wait three years to get out of her current full-time parenting situation. She is bored and needs to get back to work to feel connected to the outside world. She would eventually find a babysitter and go back to college and work.

 She was always able to laugh at our elderly parents, which made me see them in a different light, as human beings with foibles and flaws. She almost turned them into caricatures. Our father was going deaf and wanted nothing more than to get out of the house and go downtown to participate in civic affairs. He was on every planning committee and did in fact help to plan Expo 86. Mother always cut out advice articles for Rosanne and read them to her over the phone. They were usually about improving her health by quitting smoking, diet or exercise, or ways to budget and save money. She always lamented that Rosanne was hopeless with money and never made a budget or paid her bills on time. Mother was the complete opposite. She managed all the household finances because Dad was a "spendthrift" who ate "lavish lunches" out in restaurants every day at work while she always took a bag lunch. She swore that Rosanne was just like him.

# January 1987

(Envelope addressed to Buck Owens me a Letter)

Too Many Daves
Did I ever tell you of Mrs. McCave
She had twenty-three sons and named all of them Dave
Well she did, and that wasn't a smart thing to do
You see when she wants one she calls out "You-hoo"
Come into the house, she doesn't get one
All twenty-three Daves of hers come on the run!
This makes things quite difficult at the McCaves
As you can imagine with so many Daves
And so often she wishes that when they were born
She had named one of them Bodkin Van Horne
And one of them Hoos-Foos. And one of the Snimm.
And one of them Hot-Shot. And one of them Jim.
And one of them Shadrack. And one of them Blinky.
And one of them Stuffy. And one of them Stinky.
And one of them Putt-Putt. Another one Moon-Face.

*Letters From My Dead Sister*

Another one Marion O'Gravel Balloon-Face.
And one of them Ziggy. And one Soggy Muff.
One Buffalo Bill. And one Biffalo Buff.
And one of them Sneepy. And one Weepy Weed.
And one Paris Garters. And one Harris Tweed.
And one of them Michael Carmichael Zutt.
And one of them Oliver Boliver Butt.
And one of them Zanzibar Buck-Buck McFate.
But she didn't do it. And now it's too late.

By Dr. Seuss
Hey

# Note: January 1987

WHY DID SHE SEND ME THIS? PERHAPS SHE WAS DATING A GUY NAMED Dave at this time. I'm not sure. Perhaps it was a shout-out to my roommate at this time, who was named David. Was this worth the trouble of writing out by hand and mailing across Canada? Probably not, but it was amusing, nonetheless.

# Part Three

*Motherhood and Beyond*

# Coming Home

In early 1987, Rosanne left Ottawa and returned to our parents' house in Vancouver. Everything had fallen apart spectacularly after baby Michael was born. She was suffering from severe postpartum depression and Don proved himself in short order to be the useless partner and father I knew he would be. She had no choice but to put her tail between her legs and fly home into the arms of Mum, who would take care of the baby for a year while Rosanne cried and slept.

It wasn't until then that her doctor finally took this crushing postpartum depression seriously and she received effective treatment in the from of mood stabilizers that actually worked, combined with a new anti-depressant. This was life changing for her, as she could function for the first time like a regular human being, without the huge mood fluctuations. It may have literally saved her life. I don't know if she ever felt suicidal because she wouldn't have shared that with us, but there were days, weeks and even months where she was very unhappy.

I was not around home during this time, as I was still living in Montreal, and then traveling around Europe. When I did return to BC to go back to university for my teaching year, Rosanne was just starting to re-enter society and plan her next steps. She got her own apartment near our folks, collected welfare, and went back to college for a two-year psychiatric nursing diploma. She also worked part-time as a bartender, leaving the baby to sleep at Mum and Dad's, or she would get a babysitter. We reconnected during this time, and I would often visit her and the kids at the apartment for coffee before heading up to the university and it was so nice to see her coping better.

# Mum Chat
## Kitchen Nook 1987

Mum and Rosanne sat down at the orange Naugahyde kitchen nook where all important conversations took place. Mum had a cup of tea and Rosanne had coffee and a cigarette. Rosanne has been living back at home for nearly a year with her first baby son Michael after her severe bout of postpartum depression. She is doing much better now on her new medications and has found a part-time job bartending at a nearby hotel. She is ready to move on.

"So, I'm ready to start looking for an apartment for me and Mikey. I really appreciate everything you've done for me but it's time for me to move on and, like, grow a pair eh."

"How are you going to afford it?" Mum asks.

"Well, as soon as I leave here, I will qualify for welfare, based on my part-time salary and having a kid. I just need my own address to apply."

"Is that enough to live on?"

"Yah, it should be. They have promised to give me more hours soon, so that will help."

"What about babysitting? I have been minding Michael while you went to work. I'm not really prepared to come to your apartment and do this."

"I know and I would never ask you to. I have already lined up the kid sister of one of our waitresses. She is going to school and she's willing to do evenings as much as I need her because she's in high school and she's just studying anyways. All she has to do is feed Mikey and put him to bed."

"Well, that's good I suppose. But really Rosanne, this bartending is the bitter end. Don't you want to take a trades course or something to find a better career for yourself? "

"Well, I guess so, if I could do like one course at a time or something. That's all I'd have time for with work and Mikey."

"Well, Dad and I will pay for it if there's something you're interested in. Did you look at that Douglas College calendar I gave you?"

"Yah, there's a couple of things in there I liked. Psych nursing and care-aid both seemed kind of up my alley because I'm like really good with crazy old people eh."

"That sounds like a stressful career. You really want to work with people with mental issues?"

"Well I I have enough experience, don't you think?" Rosanne laughs. "I mean you and Dad are hardly normal right?"

"Go on, seriously," Mum scoffs.

"Well look at all the boyfriends I've had. Don't you think they qualify me to work with the mentally deranged?"

They both laugh. "Yeah, you may have a point," Mum says. "Well, call up an advisor on Monday and ask them about working and taking the course part-time and see what they say."

"I will. So, I found an apartment in the paper that's just down on Cottonwood Avenue that looks good. I called them and it's available for the first of next month. It's cheap and I can handle the rent, but do you think you and Dad could help me with the damage deposit?"

"How much?"

"Two-fifty."

"Probably. I'll ask Robert when he gets home."

"But wait until he's eaten dinner. Then he'll be in a better mood," Rosanne says.

"I wouldn't bank on it," Mum says. They both laugh. "But what are you going to do for furniture?"

"Well, I have everything I need for Mikey, but I was wondering if I could take the bed from downstairs?"

"Oh, all right. There's another expense because we will need to replace it in case we have guests."

"Guests? You guys never have guests."

"That's not true. We have had a few relatives visit us from Europe and we still have friends in Ontario who have threatened to come and stay."

"Okay, sorry, I guess I'll owe you for the bed. Can I take the white table and the armchair from downstairs as well? Brenda and Tom have offered me their old couch and a bedside table and Lydia's mom has a coffee table in her garage she's not using so that's really all I need."

"All right, but I'd like to have the white table back at some point because it belonged to my mother."

"Sure Mum, no problem. I'll take good care of it."

"Like hell you will. I know how you take care of things. It will be strewn with ashtrays and beer bottles in no time."

"I'll put a plastic tablecloth over it to keep it nice. Don't worry," Rosanne promises.

"All right. I suppose you need it more than we do. What about dishes?"

"I'll just get some real cheap from the thrift store down the hill. They have all kinds of dishes and cutlery. But can I take your extra drip-filter coffee pot?"

"Sure, I think I have some old sheets you can have too and an extra clock radio."

"Thanks Mum, you're the best."

"I know I am. Well, it will be good for you to have your own space again. Just don't get involved with any unsavory men. You're far better off on your own taking care of Michael and doing a college course for now. You don't need another useless man in your life taking advantage of you."

"You're right Mum, I know. I'm in no rush to be with anyone right now. I'm just glad to get out of your hair. Dad is driving me nuts. I think if I have to watch him fluff the couch cushions one more time I'm going to kill him."

"He's been very nice with Michael though. I think Michael will miss him."

"Yah, you're right. He has been pretty cute with him. Mikey loves his grandpa."

"Are you going to get some boxes from the liquor store?" Mum asks.

"I can get some from the bar. We get deliveries all the time. I'm going to call the landlord right now and tell her I'm taking the apartment."

"Okay honey. Good luck. I hope it's still available."

# Dad Chat
## Kitchen Nook 1987

Rosanne was sitting at the kitchen nook feeding baby Michael in a highchair one Saturday morning when Dad walked in wearing his baggy cotton boxers and a white cotton undershirt. He walked up to Michael and gently rubbed his head.

"How's our young man today? Is he eating well?" Dad asked, smiling.

"Yes, we really like yogurt with mashed peaches don't we Grandpa?" Rosanne replied.

Michael burbles and dribbles peaches down his chin.

"And how are you Way-Wo?" (This is how I pronounced Rosanne as a toddler, so he has always called her this, or Rosanetshuss.)

"I'm okay. I actually got eight straight hours of sleep so that's something."

Dad starts mucking about in the sink, spraying water and wiping the counter, as he did obsessively every day. Rosanne was getting annoyed.

"Why don't you sit down and have a nice cup of coffee Dad. There's still a nice piece of apple strudel in the fridge for you."

"Good idea," he got himself both and sat in his regular spot opposite her.

"So, Mum tells me you're thinking of going to Douglas College. I think that's a very good idea," he said.

"Yah, they said I can take the psych nursing program part time so that works for me. I only have to go sit in classes there one day a week for a few hours."

"When does it start?"

"In January, so I will have a bit of time to settle into my new apartment first."

"That's good. I can buy a monthly bus pass down to New Westminster for you. It stops at the bottom of 8th Street, so you just have to walk up one block."

"That would be great, thanks. I'm hoping to get a car soon. I'm getting more hours at the bar now so I can save a little each month and Laurie's dad has an old Chevelle at his gas station that he's fixing up for me. He said I could pay him $50 a month until it's paid off."

"That's very decent of him. He's a good man, that Eddie. He was a good neighbor to us too. I remember when Mum got stuck in the snow and couldn't get out of the driveway once before work and he shoveled and towed her out with his truck."

"Yah, he's a really nice guy," Rosanne said.

Rosanne got Michael out of the highchair and let him crawl off chasing the cat.

"So how do you feel about going back to school after all this time?" Dad asked.

"Fine. I'm not worried. Mum said she'd help me edit my essays so as long as I understand all the practical stuff, I should be fine. I can read fine if I can get Michael down for a long enough nap."

"That's good. I know you're smart enough to do this. You were just too distracted by boys in high school."

She laughs. "Well, that's an understatement!"

He rolls his eyes. She cleaned up the mess of baby food and pushed the highchair against the wall.

"So, who is going to help you move your stuff into the apartment?" he asks.

"Barney and Willy. Barney has his truck and there really isn't that much stuff anyways."

"You'll have to buy them some beer and a lunch. I'll give you forty dollars to cover it," he offers. "Thank you. That would really help," Rosanne said.

"Is Mum minding Michael on moving day?"

"Yah, it should only take a couple of hours. She said she would drive him over once I got his crib set up."

"Good, good. And who's this babysitter you've found to take care of him while you're at school?"

"Her name is Cindy. I work with her sister at the bar and she's in grade twelve. She wants to save up for university next year and she's willing to babysit whenever I want."

"You're lucky to have found someone like that. I hope she is responsible."

"She's very good with Michael. She came over to meet me and played with him the other day when you were at work. Mum liked her too."

"Well. if Mum likes her then she's already got the gold seal of approval," Dad smiles.

Michael has made five laps around the kitchen, dining and living rooms chasing the cat on all fours while they were chatting. Now he's got his hand in the cat food dish, so Rosanne grabs him.

"Well Dad, this boy is stinky so we're off to wash his bum, change him and get him dressed."

"What are you up to today?"

"I'm meeting Jane for coffee at the mall at eleven. We might go to the thrift store and look for some cheap dishes after."

"All right, sweetheart. I'll leave the money for the movers on the table for you. Bye-bye Michael."

He waves and Rosanne prompts Michael to wave back to Grandpa.

This was Dad at his absolute best. Sometimes he could be wonderful, especially around young children, and he was always very generous when we really needed something. Rosanne loved him deeply and I think she felt an unspoken kinship in their shared mental illness. She was as hot-headed and quick to anger as he was, but she could also be as loving and generous too. They were really two peas in a pod.

# Whistler

After Rosanne got her own apartment and was back on her feet again, Donny started making overtures to come out and join the family, but she didn't want him there. He was just a freeloader who would crash at her place and eat her food. Unfortunately, he did show up on her doorstep later that year and she was weak. Naturally, she wanted her son to know his father, especially since they looked so much alike and had the same mannerisms. She would let him sleep on the couch until he found his own place and a job. I suspected they were sleeping together occasionally, but she never let on.

During this period, I tried to get some alone time with her on several occasions. The last real quality time we spent together was when I invited her to go camping with my friends up in Whistler for the weekend. Mum and Dad offered to take toddler Michael for the weekend so that she could get a much-needed break from parenting and work.

Since I didn't own a car, Rosanne offered to drive and she sparked up a joint as we started out on the narrow, winding, perilous Sea-to-Sky highway. This already got me a little worried. We sang along to the radio until we lost reception at Lions Bay. When we stopped for lunch in Squamish, she came out of the bathroom and told me that her contact lenses had been in backwards the whole time, meaning left to right. She laughed heartily at this, and I groaned and called her an idiot. We ate our burgers and fries and got back on the road.

When we arrived at Brandywine Falls campsite, my good friends Cathy and Graham were there with their four-year-old daughter Sarah and also my long-time buddy John and his girlfriend Irene. My single friend Dave pulled up in his truck, which had a small camper in the back. Rosanne had met these people before, since I hung out with them a lot, but they didn't really know each other. We got busy pitching our tent, pulling out the gear and then walked down to put some icy river water inside the coolers to keep the beer cold. Dave started a campfire so we could roast hotdogs as an easy supper.

Rosanne immediately gravitated towards the little girl. I think she secretly always wanted a girl to make a fuss of, but alas, it wasn't in the cards. She was really good with Sarah, and they went around collecting leaves off different trees for her preschool show and tell. They were chatting the whole time as if Rosanne had known this child since birth. It was quite adorable.

Dave was really nice to Rosanne all weekend. I don't think he was trying to get laid; I think he just sensed that she was vulnerable and wanted to lift her spirits. He wasn't really flirting; he was just being his friendly self. After we sang a few songs to my guitar and taught little Sarah how to make smores, he invited Rosanne to sleep in the second bed in the camper, no strings attached, and she was thrilled to have a mattress for the night.

The next day, Dave cooked us all a bacon and egg breakfast on his little propane stove in the camper, then we hiked up to the falls and took some photos. Kathy had a good camera and got lots of shots of her daughter and husband on the rocks with the falls cascading down behind them. We took a funny group shot where Rosanne looked quite out of her element. She was not much of a nature girl and getting out into the great outdoors made her a little uncomfortable.

I was glad there was another smoker there or she would have felt embarrassed. Dave kept her company in that department. She had also never spent a weekend with just my friends, and she may have felt like an outsider. All weekend I sensed a distance between her and the rest of us, like she was off in la-la land, preoccupied. I figured it was good for her to get away from her responsibilities for a couple of days regardless.

We managed to have a pleasant weekend. She enjoyed getting into the great outdoors and liked my friends. We kept it light, got drunk around the campfire and sang old songs to my guitar. One of my fondest memories of Rosanne was the two of us singing Bobby McGee by Janis Joplin, who she always reminded me of. The combination of wildness and infinite sadness one can visibly see in this performer pretty much summed up my sister's whole being. Mix in the brazen humor and physicality of a Rosanne Barr and you've got the complete picture. Unfortunately, this would be our last weekend together, as our relationship began to unravel.

After this outing, I moved further out into the suburbs with my second husband. We were both hitting our forties. She came to see me only once in my new house and seemed quite uncomfortable the whole visit. I think she felt embarrassed by the fact that we had bought a nice new home while she was still renting with this man who she knew my parents and I hated. This would be our last attempt to maintain a friendship; we could feel ourselves growing apart.

# Good Parenting

When the boys were toddlers, she had a two-year relationship with an old acquaintance named Rob. He was much calmer and quieter than her usual choice of men, and he seemed good with the boys. He also knew many of her old friends from the neighbourhood, which was a positive. She moved into his apartment near my parents' house, and they were very happy for a couple of years. Then one day she discovered he was hiding a heroine kit in the toilet tank and was secretly a junkie. She was blown away by this and packed up her kids and left, heartbroken.

There were moments of good parenting and happy children. When they were young, with the help of our parents, the boys were enrolled in swimming lessons, pottery classes, T-ball, and Cub Scouts. She felt pride in their accomplishments and held high hopes for some sort of normal life. She loved doing crafts and coloring with them and reading them bedtime stories. She took them camping and fishing and to watch the Monster Trucks show, which they loved.

But then the flip would switch on her mood, and she would scream at them to "Fuck off!" or "Get away from me!" There was never any physical violence, but she would become depressed and disconnect physically and emotionally. She would sleep for hours and leave them to their own devices. She would drink and get high, smoking pot regularly to zone out from parenting and whatever feelings were too much to handle. Sometimes I would go over there and find her in this vegetative state, ignoring the boys, smoking endless cigarettes and staring off into space. I would suggest taking them across the street to the park to play outside and sometimes she would agree. The fresh air would help snap her back to reality and she would start talking about how her life was a mess. If she didn't have a boyfriend, she always wanted someone to come and fix everything for her by making her feel loved and hopefully bring money into her life. Being alone was a terrible place for her to be.

Because Rosanne had declared bankruptcy three times, she couldn't get a credit card for a lengthy period when her kids were little. Mum would have to bail her out whenever a larger bill arose, like a car repair or a move. She would often run out of money and call Mum for help with groceries or basic essentials for the kids. Mum was always there for her grandchildren and their relationship was fairly co-dependent. Mum was a classic enabler who never got mad and could never say no to her or her kids. I think they made her feel needed and Mum was always champion of the underdog. She always told me that I should feel sorry for Rosanne because she had such a hard life. This was baffling to me because we grew up in the exact same environment. How could we be so opposite?

When Neil was born, Mikey immediately became second fiddle and for the rest of his life she treated him as somewhat of an annoyance. This sounds harsh, but the favoritism was so obvious it was almost embarrassing. Around age eleven, Michael was deemed to be "gifted" and had a teacher who was squarely on his side, even when his behavior went off the rails at school. When he got expelled for a few days, Rosanne fiercely advocated for her son, but ended up feuding with the administration in her usual fashion. Diplomacy was not her strong suit. She became embittered and blamed the school, which didn't help her son to accept his part and move on from the incident.

The divide grew between home and school as Rosanne dug in as the opposition. Michael would later receive medication for ADD, but he had already started to feel disconnected from the whole school experience by that time. He quit school and started using drugs, which eventually led to a crystal meth addiction, damaging his brain. He lived in the forest near our mother's house for a few months after Rosanne kicked him out. Then she finally dropped him off to live on the street in a town several hundred miles away so she wouldn't have to deal with him anymore. The whole thing was a debacle that went from this happy chirping toddler wanting milk and playdough to a much slower reacting young man who finally got off the hard drugs and got the medical treatment he needed.

Her younger boy, Neil, had some learning delays due to a concussion he received from being hit by a van when he was riding his bicycle. At around age nine, he had trouble with reading and writing and Rosanne asked me to tutor him. This went quite well, and he was agreeable to receiving the extra help. However, when he got into high school, there were too many temptations and he also ended up dropping out once he got involved with selling drugs.

Rosanne really tried to be a good parent, especially when the boys were little. As her kids grew up, she gradually loosened the reins way too soon and eventually I think she gave up trying to have any control over them whatsoever. She treated them as her friends instead of her children, which backfired mightily because they grew to resent her. In their teens there was so much yelling and fighting and verbal abuse. It was a hostile environment, void of any mutual respect. I was once sick to my stomach when, at our mother's eightieth birthday in a restaurant, Neil pulled out a giant wad of drug money and refused to help his mother pay her rent. He was rude and cocky towards her and told her there was no fucking way he was going to loan her any cash. Rosanne was completely passive and emotionally beaten down. I felt so sorry for her at that moment.

I remember when my husband was called by Grandma at three in the morning to pick the boys up from jail. When he arrived at the police station, the cop was visibly disappointed. He asked, "Why did you come?" He wanted them to stay in jail for the night to simmer down and possibly learn a lesson. My husband got nothing but verbal abuse from the back of the car all the way to their home. When he dropped them off, he said Rosanne was the most intoxicated he had ever seen her. Her place was a complete mess, and she didn't even thank him for driving them across the city in the middle of the night, when she knew he had to work the next morning. The boys immediately started yelling at her that they were going back out to the same party where they had just been arrested and then slammed their bedroom doors behind them. My husband said he had never realized how dysfunctional her home life was until he saw this scene.

Should I have stepped up to be a better Auntie to her children? Undoubtedly, yes. I was selfish with my youth and my time and also very much a realist as to whether I could make a difference in the trajectory of their lives. Rosanne took every opportunity to blame me for failing her and her children. She wanted me to be the type of life partner she needed: a strong role model and disciplinarian; a solid financial provider; and a good-natured pick-me-up when she was feeling blue. I wanted none of these responsibilities. I had my own circle of friends, and I was into university, working out, partying, travel, and eventually marriage, my own kids, and my teaching career. Her whole situation seemed impossibly draining to me. Perhaps I was selfish, but I never bought into the whole victim card she was playing. She grew up in the same house as me with the same parents and opportunities.

I didn't really understand how much of an impairment her mental illness was. There wasn't the same public awareness about mental health back in the sixties and seventies as there is now. I understand now that her depression and mood disorder prevented her from making positive choices. Back then, I believed that once she was on medication, she should have been fixed, but this wasn't the case. I knew that her antidepressants stopped working for her several times, so she needed to switch brands and readjust. However, I couldn't feel sorry for her because of her abject refusal to seek counseling or professional psychiatry. She always thought she knew better than the professionals. Perhaps this was out of fear of being called out on her substance abuse and addictions.

# The Joe Years

When Rosanne was thirty, she moved into a small rental house with her two small boys. She needed a regular babysitter and found a young woman barely twenty years old named Kristen, who was willing to work either day or night shifts at her place. They hit it off and became good friends who would smoke a joint together after she got home from work.

Kristen had a boyfriend who was exactly Rosanne's type; a short, stocky, swarthy man with a giant chip on his shoulder and a muscle car. The three of them became good friends and Kristen was really good with her boys. One day, disaster struck as Joe got into a serious car accident and Kristen was killed. Rosanne and Joe were both devastated, but they bonded over their shared grief and eventually fell in love.

This began the saga of a fifteen-year disastrous relationship where I helped her move six times to get away from Joe, who was verbally abusive, but Rosanne swore it was never physical. We never saw bruises, but I still have my doubts. Every time she left him, he would hound her until she would cave and let him back in. It was a cycle where she would call our mother, who would call me and ask if I could help her move yet again. We would advise her ad nauseum to leave him once and for all, but she hated our advice and refused to go to a professional counselor, believing since she had taken psychology at college, that she knew better about herself than anyone else. This stubbornness was exasperating. We had to watch her spiral back down into the heartache every time that man drew her back in and treated her like shit. It was such a hopeless cycle.

Of course, her kids also suffered too. As Rosanne moved from one apartment to the next in order to get away from Joe, her sons knew a life of instability. I don't know if they ever really felt emotionally connected to him or upset about her moving on. They managed to stay fairly close to our parents' neighborhood so they could stay in the same schools and visit Grandma and Grandpa

Being moved from place to place, they had to adjust to constant change, and they learned not to trust the man in her life. When she was working night shifts as a bartender, closing the bar and getting home around two in the morning, the boys were left to fend for themselves. After they got home from school, she would leave after cooking them dinner. They were entirely free to entertain their friends and get into all kinds of trouble. After finishing college, she began psych nursing and would often work the graveyard shift, giving them free run of the place all night. This was a recipe for disaster as they got older, and school became less and less important.

As they grew into young teens, their behaviour went off the rails and they started using and dealing drugs and hanging out with likeminded friends. Rosanne had difficulty controlling them and pretty much let them run wild. They both eventually dropped out of school. The icing on the cake was Joe stealing money off one of her boys, which created a rift and more infighting.

The relationship between Rosanne and her sons was becoming really toxic. There was so much yelling and verbal abuse that I couldn't stand being around them anymore. The brothers would often fight and even pulled knives on each other once and the cops were called. Rosanne was losing control, so she eventually gave up and allowed them to set up a grow op in her place. I remember going over there to find a bunch of pot plants and grow lights right out in the open beside the kitchen. Apparently, she was happy to get a free or "deep discount" supply of weed for herself if she turned a blind eye. There was less animosity between her and the boys if she just let them do whatever they wanted.

During this period of her life, she alienated me by staying with Joe and creating such a toxic home environment that I couldn't stand to be around her or her kids anymore. I didn't want to expose my own children to this lifestyle and became very protective. There were so many scary incidents with her boys that I refused to put myself or my kids in harm's way. My daughter was six and my stepson was ten and this was the worst possible influence for any child. Rosanne couldn't understand why I didn't want to see her anymore and resented me for distancing myself. This is when our relationship ended.

My anger grew when our father died and her boys started taking advantage of our mother as well, who was approaching eighty years old. When her eldest son started cooking and using crystal meth, Rosanne couldn't handle them anymore and sent them to live at Grandma's. I was furious. They set up a grow-op in her basement and all kinds of bad things started happening. They put a lock on the rec room door so she couldn't access this part of her own house. My naïve mother thought they just wanted their privacy. When there was a break-in, Mum paid a lot of money to have bars installed over her windows.

Finally, after pleading with Rosanne to rectify this outrageous situation in a detailed letter I left in her mailbox, she told her eldest to leave. It was still an awful situation. The younger one stayed on and continued his illicit dealings, while making it uncomfortable for me to visit my own mother, threatening me and my husband every time we came by.

It didn't help that grandma was a pushover, who would never stand up for herself. Our mother would say that it wasn't such a big deal and enabled this bad behavior. She always took the side of the boys, viewing them as underdogs and feeling sorry for them and for Rosanne for having such a hard life. Sometimes I felt like the enemy for trying to protect her. It was a wretched situation to be in and I placed the blame squarely on Rosanne. I was not sympathetic to her plight, and she always felt that I judged her too harshly. She tended to view herself as a victim of circumstance and never took responsibility for making any poor choices. Perhaps if her kids weren't exposed to a revolving door of terrible men, they could have turned out differently. I think our father was the only positive male role model they ever had in their lives because he would at least yell at them and correct them when they stepped out of line. But as he got old, he couldn't cope with their antics anymore.

The neighbour's houses started getting robbed, and there were incidents of violence around Neil where he was hiding from different people and parking his car down the street to avoid detection. Once, there were even bullet holes in his car. He came home scared one night and said he had been kidnapped and beaten up for hours and his truck stolen. He was obviously involved with some very dangerous people and in way over his head. I was very afraid for my mother's safety. This was the last straw for me in trying to have any relationship with Rosanne. I couldn't accept that she had put our old mother in harm's way.

# Prison

FINALLY, JOE GOT ARRESTED FOR SOME SERIOUS CRIME AND WAS SENT to prison on Vancouver Island. He had already killed her beloved young babysitter several years before in a car accident and was charged with manslaughter, so this was his second strike. He was sentenced to fifteen years. The most sickening part was seeing my sister catch a ferry to visit him. She even made an effort and kept in touch with his family back east to keep that relationship going.

Rosanne would drive for a couple of hours, catch the ferry to Vancouver Island, then drive some more to visit Joe in prison. Once, she even ran into my father-in-law, who was also there visiting a friend. He saw her across the visiting room and asked:

"Hey, don't I know you?"

"Yah, you're my sister Nam's husband's father, right?"

"Oh Yah, I met you at their wedding. So, who are you visiting?"

"My boyfriend," she must have said with some degree of embarrassment- or not- depending on her mood that day. "How 'bout you?"

"Oh, he's one of my oldest friends. He just can't stay out of trouble."

"I know what you mean," said Rosanne.

"Well good to see you again. Take care. Say hi to Nam for me."

"Sure, likewise."

She came home from the visit and reported to Mum that Joe was building a beautiful cedar box in his native tradition for her to keep his belongings in at her place. She then dutifully called his mother in Ontario to report on her visit and chat because they were friendly.

"He looks good," she would tell her. "He's been working out a lot and learning how to cook. He's working in the kitchen and planning to do a vocational chef's course when he gets out on probation. They are placing him in a halfway house downtown for the first couple of months during this retraining." She was full of unbridled optimism for her man.

Then, when he was finally released, he went straight into that cooking class, met another woman, and married her two weeks later. Rosanne was mortified. Here she was, waiting for this asshole for years on end, only to be betrayed by him in the most flagrant possible way. It was an unbearable humiliation. She became angry and then depressed, and unfortunately, this turned out to be the last long-term relationship of her life. She tried some online dating later on, but it never amounted to much. He stole ten to fifteen prime years of her life and her boys hated him. He had even stolen money from them at one point.

Joe's relationship with the new woman was short lived because he got arrested again for another crime and put back in a higher-security prison in Ontario. Shortly after his incarceration, he killed himself in prison. I wonder how Rosanne felt when she heard the news. She probably felt bad for his mother and called her up to commiserate. That is just the kind of person she was. She would put her own needs on the backburner and find a way to connect to the suffering of others. She was very compassionate that way.

The whole debacle was a tragedy from start to finish and I always wished better for her, even though I had no contact with her during this period. I heard all this second-hand from our mother, who understandably felt powerless to convince Rosanne to forget about this loser and choose a better partner for herself. A better partner would have been anyone with a pulse, but there was no convincing Rosanne of anything-ever. She would stubbornly forge ahead with blinders on and the more advice she heard, the more she pushed back. It was better for us to say nothing. Mum would always be her port of call in the storm of her life.

# Young Adults

When Michael returned from his two years living on the streets, he was clean, however he was brain damaged. His speech was slower and his whole demeanor had changed. He agreed to see a psychiatrist to get treatment for ADD and, presumably, his addictions as well. He started turning a corner and became more cooperative with his mother. They rebuilt their damaged relationship, and he tried his hand at several jobs.

He got into a relationship with a very young woman who got pregnant. She bore him a son, who he was only allowed to see a few times before she moved on to a new man and forbade him any contact. Rosanne never got to spend any time with this grandson, and she never talked about him but I'm sure she must have felt some disappointment around the whole ordeal. Perhaps she was also relieved that the girl never came after Michael for child support payments, which he didn't have.

As an adult, Michael found a better life for himself. He now lives on a First Nations reserve with his wife and two children in a remote part of British Columbia and is working on fishing boats. From what I've seen, there is still plenty of disharmony in his day-to-day relationship, but overall he seems to have found a place of acceptance in a big extended family who love and take care of him. I am happy for him.

Neil's life never seemed like he came from our middle-class suburban neighborhood; it sounded more like life in "the projects" of a major American city. At one point we found bullets buried under the floorboards in my dead father's closet. I know there were times when Neil was genuinely scared for his life. If he hadn't been so consistently hostile towards me, I might even have felt sorry for him. He was a young man who got into "the life" way too young and when he wanted out, it was a struggle to extricate himself from all the people around him.

For years I lived in fear of him. When my husband and I moved into the house with my Mum in her final years, he continued to threaten us every time he came by. He would literally say, "I'm going to kill you!" He hated the fact that we lived with his grandma because he didn't want to deal with seeing us there or having to make the effort to be civil when he clearly hated my guts. He saw us as "the haves" and his mother, Rosanne, as the family victim because she had always portrayed herself this way. She always blamed her failures on us instead of taking any responsibility for the life choices she had made, and her son believed this to be true.

Neil blamed me for the estrangement between Rosanne and I and he was generally angry at the world, with a hair-trigger temper and no impulse control. He perceived the breakdown of our relationship as me cutting Rosanne off because I thought she wasn't good enough. In reality, I mostly stopped seeing her because of him. I couldn't stand being around this belligerent teenager, young man and then full adult. I started purposefully leaving whenever he was coming to visit our mother to avoid having to deal with him. When I knew he was coming, my heart would race and my blood-pressure would spike, giving me terrible headaches, so I would go for a drive and have Mum call me when he was gone. The whole experience was exacerbated by Mum's constant denial of his aggression. She would tell me that he had a hard life, and I should be nicer to him because he was just misunderstood. I know that she loved her grandson, but she was also frustratingly naive.

Fortunately, all men grow up at some point and it took until about age thirty for them to find steady employment, settle down with decent women and start their own families. They always went back to their mother and grandmother to visit regularly. Grandma was always the rock, providing unconditional love, wisdom, a hot meal, and financial support. She was steady, grounded and predictable; all the things that Rosanne was not. Rosanne had always wished to have boys she could party with, and her wish came true. Unfortunately, this wasn't a recipe for great parenting; she was the fun mother, not the stable one and she wasn't very good at setting the boundaries that kids need.

After my sister died, when her sons were in their thirties and had young children of their own, I managed to have a positive dialogue with them while I was acting as executrix for her estate. Things were settled amicably, and we have all moved on with our own separate lives. Somehow all children eventually grow up and figure things out. I'm sure the death of their mother and grandmother within the space of a year was a sobering reality for them both. I wish them and their families only peace and happiness.

# Our Father's Passing

It became abundantly clear, when our dad was dying in hospital, just how much my sister was emotionally attached to him. Suddenly I could understand her claims that her promiscuity was due to a deep-seated fear of abandonment originating when she was a little girl because he frequently traveled on business. This made no sense to me when I first read her self-analysis in a college psychology essay. It didn't ring true.

Our father's nervous breakdown after Rosanne was born may have created some unconscious perception of him as withdrawing from her. Perhaps there was a lack of bonding that made her more needy for male attention, but I am no psychologist. All I know is, her relationships with men throughout her life were unhealthy. She always put up with way too much crap and acted uncharacteristically submissive. I get a sense of this in the letters from Ottawa, when she is making Don's work lunches and dinners before she goes off to work and complains about how he never shares his money with her. He goes out with other people on his days off and blows all his cash getting drunk and high. She just accepts all this and rolls over, even dolling herself up with make-up before he arrives home from work to make herself more sexually appealing to him. It was a pitiful display from someone who was usually powerfully assertive in public.

This dual public-private personality seemed indicative of chronically low self-esteem. The loud, vulgar bravado in public hid this very well. Most people thought she was fierce and wouldn't take shit from anyone. Meanwhile, at home, she was internally trying to be "the little woman" to the men who never respected her intellect or her strong work ethic. These men continually took advantage of her both sexually and financially. She dated a long list of couch surfing freeloaders who were not very nice to her. It never got to physical abuse, except perhaps with Joe, which I cannot confirm. Once, during one of her rushed moves to a new home, Mom said he had hit her. This is where Rosanne finally drew the line, thank god.

We had never been physically abused at home. Rosanne and I both knew instinctively that no matter how psychologically damaged our father was, he loved us and would never hurt us. He came home every night hurling verbal abuse at my mother for not cleaning the house or cooking the right food or simply rage against his present circumstances, but he never raised a hand to her or us. He was really a gentle, damaged man and would sometimes make up cute little bedtime stories for us as kids. He loved animals especially, and would be so tender with them, taking us to the petting zoo or just cuddling our own five cats. He was also deeply moved by orchestral music because his father had been a concert cellist. He would often cry at the symphony, which helped me to see through his angry exterior into his damaged soul.

As teenagers, Rosanne and I were oblivious to the trauma our father must have experienced at the loss of his parents and how deeply psychologically damaged he was. We both realized as adults, that we had been completely selfish and intolerable towards our father as adolescents. I think we regretted all the horrible things we said to him back then. We finally felt compassion for the terrible hardship he had lived through in WWII.

When our father died in hospital at age eighty-two of undiagnosed and sudden internal bleeding, my husband reported to me how Rosanne crumbled into a mess, sobbing at his bedside. I had chosen not to be there because I had visited him the previous day and he had smiled at me when I put ice chips in his mouth and that's how I wanted to remember him. She wore his gold and ruby pinky ring for the rest of her life. She seemed to feel a much deeper loss at his passing than I, or even our mother, did. I mostly felt relief that our mother could live her final years in peace. She was an inherently happy person and I intended to help her enjoy the rest of her life to the fullest.

Unfortunately, Rosanne started taking our parents' treasured belongings out of the house without asking me whenever she would stop by to visit Mum. Mum was usually complicit in this because she always felt sorry for Rosanne. She treated her as the underdog our whole lives and enabled most of her disruptive behavior. In fact, I think Mum secretly got a kick out of Rosanne being naughty and sticking it to me whenever she got the chance.

She took all the antique Christmas decorations from our grandparents and all the handmade stuffed toys our grandmother had made by hand. She took artwork: the Dutch plates; the giant Dutch sailing ship painting; the gold-framed eighteenth-century English pastoral; the Japanese panther print; all the antique prints of lawyers in their robes; the Matisse-like still-life. She took Dad's mahogany and red velvet armchair, all the First Nations baskets and our terrific seashell collection, the nineteenth century long-handled copper bed warmer pan and all the decorative German household china. She took Grandma's knitted Afghan blanket; the mid-century wooden desk chairs, the folding woven macrame chair. She also took the only framed photo of our German grandparents, and both of the large, framed photos of Dad as a little boy in a sailor suit sitting on his father's lap. Mum's handpainted jewelry chest disappeared and then I was told that I could have the ugly utilitarian campaign chest to even the score.

I was given a couple of things: the family silverware and English china set; one Dutch glass windmill painting that I cherished; Grandmother's clock and the old push-button radio. After seeing all Rosanne's pilfering, I also squirreled away one antique wooden spice canister that I particularly liked. After I moved in with Mum, I made a conscientious effort to divide up the photo albums equally, splitting all our childhood photos carefully so that she would get most of the photos showing her as a child and teenager and all the ones with her children in them. She also got all the old German family photo albums, as per Mum's wishes.

I don't really care about all this stuff; other than the way it was taken. It was as if Mum and Rosanne were in cahoots and plotting against me to make things gradually disappear so that I wouldn't notice. It felt like a surreptitious act of complicity against me. It seemed like every time Rosanne came over, something else was missing from the walls. Mum would always say, "Oh Naomi, you've got everything going for you. Rosanne is so hard-done-by. Just let her have it."

This was the dynamic of my life. I was always the responsible child, and she was always the needy child and that's just the way it was. Every family has its own dynamic that becomes entrenched in the psyches and behaviors of its members, and this was ours. We were blessed that our mother gave us all these things well before she died so there wouldn't be any feuding, since Rosanne and I were already long estranged at this point. However, I'm frustrated now that I do not have a single photo of my German grandparents.

# Battles

Rosanne had at least two huge battles with her employers. They both arose from accusations of impropriety at work, which she adamantly fought. I'm not sure what the first incident was but the second incident involved a First Nations woman accusing Rosanne of pushing her down when the patient tried to use the phone without permission. She got her union to back her up, but it was a long-drawn-out process in both cases. She never felt fully supported by her union reps. She ended up going through massively stressful hearings and leaving her jobs both times. The second one ended her career, and she ended up going on long-term medical disability.

At this point, Rosanne had moved farther away from us to buy her first home on the Sunshine Coast to try and make a fresh start. I would always hear reports from my mother on how she was faring now that her kids were grown and had moved out. She seemed happier to be living up there, away from the big city of Vancouver. She enjoyed the quieter small-town life.

She went through a court battle when one of her son's dogs bit a woman on the beach and Rosanne fought to keep the dog from being put down. She lost both the court case and the dog in the end. This was a very stressful and upsetting time for her.

Then there were Rosanne's three oldest female friendships that broke down. One by one Lydia, Brenda, and Mary all stopped calling her and she was devastated each time. Her public expression was always one of anger. "Fuck her if she can't take a joke!" But underneath the surface there was great hurt and sadness. She may have reflected on what her own part in the split might have been, but she never expressed this, she always blamed the other party for doing her wrong. She vowed to move on and forget all about them, but easier said than done.

Our own relationship breakdown and estrangement had started when she let Joe move back in for the sixth time. I had basically given up at this point. Our mother always placed the blame squarely on me for not being compassionate enough. It was always, "Poor Rosanne," and, "What could I do to fix it?" My husband finally had to explain to Mum, in her old age, some of the issues we had dealt with over the years, such as Rosanne's son threatening to kill us repeatedly. Mum would never believe these things when I told her, nor take me seriously, but she would listen to my husband.

Rosanne accused me of ripping her off when I bought her out of her half of our parents' home and decided to move in and care for Mum for her last ten years. I offered Rosanne the opportunity to do this several times, but she said she wanted no part of that house. My husband even pulled her aside and told her not to take the deal because the value of the house would go up, but she adamantly wanted to take the money and run. It was a fair deal at the time, and we signed the contract, but she bitched about it for years later and blamed me for everything.

I had reached out several times, inviting her to visit or come for Christmas dinner. I always invited her to stay with Mum whenever we went away on vacation so they could have some quality time together. I would only see her occasionally at our parents' home for a quick cup of tea and it always felt tense and forced. We could manage to keep things civil with Mum and my husband acting as buffers, but that was the extent of it. All serious topics of discussion were avoided, and we kept it light and jocular. We still knew how to make each other laugh and there were a few moments that reminded me of how we used to be.

This rift between us lasted for the rest of her life. She held onto so much bitterness, believing that I had rejected her as a person because I didn't want to spend time with her and her family. My husband and I were simply not willing to accept the verbal abuse anymore, which made it even harder to rekindle any kind of relationship. There were moments when we gathered to celebrate Mum's birthday, but they were short and uncomfortable. We had been so close in our youth, and it all fell apart, but I have made my peace with it. She chose her path, and I chose mine. Such is life.

At times she felt lonely and attempted online dating. She met one fellow who was older than her and in poor health. Apparently, during one of their early visits, he dropped dead on her kitchen floor. Then she got into a relationship with a wealthy man from Germany who flew over to see her. She didn't know he was married at the time, but I'm assuming this is what ended it. Once she agreed to meet a man who turned out, by coincidence, to be her best friend Jenna's plumber. Imagine Jenna's surprise when they walked in together to her New Year's party. It was their first date and Jenna later reported that Rosanne unceremoniously dumped him after this one night out because he wouldn't sleep with her.

Her old boyfriend Bob resurfaced when Rosanne was alone in her fifties. She got a phone call one day from him and agreed to meet up. They had one visit and she reported back to Mum that she couldn't be with a man who had no teeth. She wouldn't have minded if he had dentures, but he was actually walking around with no teeth, and this was apparently where she drew the line. It was probably an indication that he had no money to pay for any dentures and she was done with freeloaders at this stage of her life. She probably couldn't forgive his past transgressions either. It's a shame because she was lonely, and he would have made a nice companion.

Rosanne never would get married in her lifetime. In the end, she was alone and lonely for some male companionship. Honestly, I don't think she ever found a man she could really talk to as a friend and an equal partner. There was always some kind of disconnect where she became the caregiver, and they became the user.

When she was diagnosed with breast cancer and had a unilateral mastectomy, we invited her to stay with us post-surgery because it was the best option for her in the city near the hospital. We doted on her and brought her treats. She was friendly during this time, and she always liked my husband, who still served as a buffer between us. She refused the spare bed and crashed on the couch, sprawled out smoking cigarettes in the living room watching TV. I had to tell her to put underwear on because she was displaying her bare crotch to my husband as she snored loudly. We even managed to have a few laughs during this visit. She was tough as nails, and never complained about the pain or expressed any feelings of self-pity over the loss of her breast. She was determined to get on with her life.

I still don't know why she opted out of chemotherapy or radiation. She chose instead to be part of a clinical drug trial, using some kind of pills instead to prevent the cancer from returning. This worked for a year or two, but then the cancer metastasized into her lungs and spine, and she was in a bad state. Thankfully she had three devoted friends who stepped up to help her during this time. They drove her to appointments and kept our aged mother apprised of what was happening. Her sons helped out as well but were living quite far away.

When Mum was in her nineties, I suggested to Rosanne via email that she might eventually need to go into a care home. Rosanne fired off a slew of angry replies. She concluded that Mum should go and stay with her, which was ridiculous because Mum couldn't even manage the steps into her home by that point, never mind being removed from her doctors and other supports. Rosanne was already really sick by this point and could barely care for herself. She had not taken part in our mother's care for the previous ten years, but felt the sudden need to weigh in. She was just throwing barbs at me as a last-ditch effort to say she cared about Mum.

# Beach Walks

Rosanne's last few years were very quiet and sometimes lonely. She returned to crafting, making some paper mâché plates and bowls, weaving placemats, and constructing artsy pieces from driftwood. She also enjoyed gardening when she had the energy and would often confer with Mum by phone about plants and their preferred conditions. She loved watching tennis on TV, like my mother, and they would remind each other of upcoming tournaments. She also watched baseball. She was brave enough to get a bathing suit with a built-in prosthetic breast to go swimming at the pool.

She could spend her days happily scouring vintage and antique shops for strange and beautiful objects. She had always loved browsing in little crafty shops, so in my mind I picture her choosing a pink ceramic flower vase at the local thrift shop to arrange her garden blooms. She also loved collecting baskets and had some splendid First Nations pieces.

Her dress was still eccentric. She wore big chunky jewelry, jungle prints, loose fitting handmade woolen cardigans, and funky felt hats. She loved make-up and would accentuate her big brown eyes with a thin sweep of eyeliner and lots of mascara. She looked terrific in reddish-brown lipstick and rouge, which she applied tastefully. When she was younger, she wore foundation make-up because she didn't like the larger pores around her nose. She could be quite put-together at times but could also be slovenly when her mood was low. She had no qualms about going out in sweats and flip-flops if she wasn't 'feeling it'. She was real to the max and lived by the motto "What you see is what you get." She refused to put on airs for anyone. Rosanne had always admired saucy, fearless women who, like herself, lived outside the margins of society and made their own rules. She would have made a fine poet if she had ever applied herself to her writing.

For several years, near the end of her life, she drove around proudly in a smashed-in vehicle. It was like her badge of honor calling out to the world, "Look at me! I'm fucked! I have cancer and the whole world can go to hell!" She became more disheveled after she got sick and started taking more pills. She sometimes appeared like she'd just crawled out of bed and had forgotten to brush her hair, which of course is understandable considering what she was going through.

She would have also been on the lookout for small gifts for her three baby grandchildren, whom she doted on whenever she got the chance. She was naturally friendly and chatty with shopkeepers and I'm sure all the local vendors knew her in such a small town. In my imagination, I see her as being well-liked and treated with kindness wherever she went in those final years. I would hope that the fiery temper and lippy sarcastic comebacks would have cooled with her illness, but of course this may not have been the case. Serious illness sometimes makes people more cantankerous, but I choose to remember her in an easier peaceful light. Perhaps this is just my coping mechanism for dealing with my own guilt at not being there for her in her hour of need.

I have numerous friends who are lonely now. I recognize it when they dominate our conversations because they haven't had anyone to listen to them for a long while. They also frequently sleep on the couch with the lights on and the TV blaring, as Rosanne did, so they feel like someone else is watching over them. I know our mother was always there to listen and I hope Rosanne had others in her small community to chat with in person. As much as we didn't get along, I always wished her a happy life and hated to think she was isolated and suffering.

# Travel

It always surprised me that Rosanne never did much traveling after Ottawa. She wasn't particularly outdoorsy, but she took her boys camping once in Tofino when they were young. If she traveled by car, it was usually to visit someone and stay at their place for a few days. She was an incredibly social creature. Like many people, I suppose she became bogged down in the routines of work and motherhood and lost sight of any bigger travel dreams she may have had.

Even though we had relatives she could have stayed with in several European countries, she never went abroad to visit them. I don't think it was for lack of funds because our parents would have helped her get there if she were really keen. I think there was an underlying lack of self-esteem that held her back. Perhaps she felt lesser than because our relatives were all university educated and she wasn't. She probably thought our parents had written negative things in their correspondence about her wild teenage years, that her reputation would precede her and prejudiced them against her. Perhaps she felt some shame about what she'd put our parents through. This is all conjecture on my part. Perhaps she simply lacked the self-confidence to deal with foreign languages, currencies, and navigation, but something held her back.

I was pleased that she finally got to take a trip to Mexico after her first round of cancer treatment. She had met a woman in her cancer support group who she felt comfortable with, basking in the sun together for a week. This was both her first and last tropical getaway. I hope she had a lovely time.

# Jenna Stories 2

Rosanne and Jenna remained friends throughout their lives and Jenna ended up caring for her through her cancer treatments. She let her stay over when she needed to come into the city, drove her to appointments and took notes to help her manage her medications. This sometimes resulted in arguments because Rosanne wasn't always an easy person to help. She would sometimes get angry if Jenna tried to talk sense into her and then give her the silent treatment for days.

Jenna knew all her pill-popping habits, which had been going on for years. After the "bennies" of her youth, she became particularly fond of Percocet and Ativan and would often drive while taking these, against all doctor's advice. This is probably why the side of her vehicle was caved in, which she wore like a badge of honor as if to say, "Fuck you!" to the world at large.

On top of these she would take any number of generic painkillers like Tylenol, Ibuprofen or Aspirin. She had no issue with smoking, drinking or smoking pot on top of these doses. It's a miracle her organs held out for as long as they did. She had the constitution of a horse.

Jenna had always kept in touch with Mum, but as Rosanne lost her grip on reality, Jenna began reaching out to me and to her other caregiver friends, Alison and Arlene as well. They would swap stories on how things were going and help each other to cope with Rosanne's tantrums. Jenna explained how, at one of her medical appointments, Rosanne had purposefully taken fourteen two-ninety-two painkillers in front of the reception nurse just to get her attention. Perhaps she was feeling unseen or unvalidated by the cancer clinic on that particular day. The nurse told her that if she carried on that way, her kidneys would fail and she would die. Poor Jenna had to admonish her on the way home, only to be met with some choice words.

On one visit to the cancer clinic, Rosanne was told to wait for a scan and she lost her patience.

"I'm not waiting!" she announced.

"Yes, you damn well are!" Jenna said. "I didn't drive you all the way out here to leave without this scan. Sit your ass down and quit throwing a hissy-fit."

Rosanne returned to her chair and sulked. Thank goodness Jenna could put her in her place if necessary.

Another time, Jenna had to call the police in Vancouver to alert them to her driving when she sounded completely incoherent on the phone. They pulled her over and impounded her vehicle. By the time Alison drove all the way into the city to pick her up, Rosanne had already left on a bus to get back to the ferry. She was fuming mad at Jenna for ratting her out and couldn't see that Jenna had very possibly saved her life or someone else's.

We knew that Rosanne had opted for pills as the course of treatment for her cancer. However, Jenna shared with me that Rosanne had been offered and refused chemo and radiation, which Mum and I were not aware of. Apparently, Rosanne's friend Arlene from her local cancer support group told Jenna that one woman in their circle was touting an all-natural approach to treatment and Rosanne bought into it, which I cannot believe. Rosanne was so pro-pharmaceuticals, but maybe she was afraid of chemo.

I am so grateful to these three women friends who stepped up to support Rosanne in her hour of need when I couldn't or wouldn't. Yes, there is some shame in my own failure to step up, but I truly believe that Rosanne would have pushed me away had I offered. I realize how lame this sounds now as I write it. I guess I will never know. Jenna was her most patient and caring friend and Rosanne was so very lucky to have her. I hope she found some occasions to thank her along the way, but it's doubtful.

Her one bright light during these treatment years was the arrival of grandchildren. Her eldest had two babies, a boy and a girl, and her youngest had a son. She loved it when they visited and would make a fuss over them with whatever energy she had. She even found the strength to drive up to the First Nations reserve where her eldest lived with his wife to visit over Christmas. This must have been a Herculean feat for someone so sick and showed how much she cared.

During one of her treatments in the city, she came and stayed with Mum for a week while we took a vacation. After she left, we found different coloured pills all over the floor and realized the extent to which she was self-dosing different pharmaceuticals. Perhaps this was an attempt to overdose on her darker days. It was tragic to know that she was suffering and in pain. Our whole family often felt powerless to try and help her, especially our mother. Even in her nineties, she was still making calls to get police over to Rosanne's house to check up on her and make sure she was alive and safe. She never, ever gave up on her. Once, my mother called them to get her off the road after Rosanne had sounded impaired on the phone. This was a very upsetting period, during which we wondered if she might take her own life; we were always on high alert when the phone rang.

After one of these phone calls to Mom where Rosanne sounded completely incoherent and was crying a lot, we consulted with her two closest friends who were helping with her care. Then my aged mother called the police to get her a ride to the psych unit at her nearest hospital. She was admitted and then soon transferred to a better equipped city hospital. She remained there for a month or two while they got her medications back in check and weaned her off the ones she was abusing. She became lucid again and joined the land of the living. It was a scary time. Her boys were summoned to visit her, but she was too embarrassed to have me drive mum there and bring her up in her wheelchair. Mum didn't really want to go either, to be honest. She felt overwhelmed with going out anywhere at this point and also powerless to help her. And Rosanne certainly didn't want to see me.

Her sons were helpful when she was sick, but they lived further away and had difficulty getting to her quickly when she needed them. Neil also took her in overnight sometimes, would drive up to visit her, fix her car, and do repairs around her house. Michael did the best he could from a distance with a young family to look after and he was often out on fishing boats where we couldn't reach him by phone.

During another one of Rosanne's physical setbacks near the end of her life, she was admitted to hospital in the city. Fearing that she was nearing the end, I decided to go and see her and brought her a small gift. When I arrived, she had another friend in the room, so I didn't stay. I quickly told her I was sorry she was suffering and that I loved her and left the small Buddha statue containing an orchid on her side table. Rosanne was still angry at me and started to cry, telling me I should do the right thing, by which she meant giving her boys money. She still felt that the deal we had made over our parents' estate was unfair, even though she agreed to it ten years before and signed a legal contract. I went to the car and cried, knowing this would probably be the last time I'd see her.

The cancer battle dragged on, first with a mastectomy and then, after it metastasized, she fought for almost two more years. Rosanne died at age sixty, with her boys by her bedside. My ninety-four-year-old Mum was still alive, and I spent the day consoling her at her care home. She was always stoic, but we both cried that day, and I was so touched when the sweet Filipino nurse came in and gave Mum a hug. It's never easy to lose a child, even when you're very old.

Because Rosanne had been sick and in pain for a long time, her death came as somewhat of a relief to both Mum and I because her suffering had ended. There may have been some peace for Mum in knowing that she was finally free from pain.

# After Rosanne's Passing

I HAVE KEPT IN TOUCH WITH ROSANNE'S FRIENDS JENNA AND LYDIA since she passed, and we swap stories and laugh about the good old times. Jenna moved closer to me and because they were lifelong friends from the age of twelve, she knew our whole family well. She has photos of Rosanne from the seventies. We get together from time to time and share memories of their wilder days and also the terrible final years. Jenna really stepped up in her hour of need and I am so grateful to her.

The second woman who helped Rosanne in her final two years was her work friend Alison, who had a young son with special needs. I never got to know her and only met her twice, but both these women were saints in my eyes. They were the very definition of unconditional love, stepping up when Rosanne was at her lowest and opening their arms and their homes. I hope to have such friends show up in my hour of need. She was so very lucky to have such a caring work colleague.

Mum didn't stay depressed after the initial tears over Rosanne's death. She just soldiered on and died one year later, almost to the day. I hope they are happy together somewhere having a nice cup of tea and laughing.

My immediate birth family was suddenly all gone, and I felt

untethered, like I had no home. I remember driving a year later and suddenly feeling totally disoriented, like I had no idea where home was anymore. I started crying for no logical reason. I couldn't even put into words what was wrong. I realized that my only living relatives who I had contact with were my two first cousins in England and my daughter. Thank goodness my husband had a large family, or I would have been very lonely indeed. For the first time I understood how people can be truly alone in the world.

# Celebration of Life

Her celebration of life took me by surprise. I had been reluctant to attend due to my ongoing bad relationship with my nephews, but I'm very glad I went. I took my husband and Rosanne's dear friend Jenna, partly to act as buffers for my interactions with her sons. Unfortunately, Mum couldn't attend. She was ninety-four and refused to leave the care home in a wheelchair because she had great anxiety about going out anywhere, which was understandable. I also believe she didn't want to be seen upset and crying in public.

Rosanne's younger son organized it and it turned out extremely well. It was a beautiful day, held in a community hall by the ocean. There was a table of photographs and her son had put together a slideshow of her life. People were milling about swapping stories, fawning over the children, and when asked to be seated, they nearly filled the long tables. There was ample food for everyone.

I was amazed by the turnout. There were a bunch of nurses there from her old job at the forensic psych prison, where she hadn't worked for at least ten years. Where were all these women while she was going through her dispute with management? Rosanne never mentioned having any moral support through this difficult process. We had the impression that she felt very alone, but obviously there were many co-workers who really cared about her. I only knew of one work friend who had stood by her through thick and thin and helped her through her cancer treatment as well. I thanked her for all her efforts to help Rosanne cope with everything life threw at her.

There was also her old friend Jane who came down from the Yukon to attend and this really touched me. They had obviously kept in touch since high school and she was one of the only girlfriends, other than Jenna, who had stuck by her from that early period of her life. It was heartwarming to talk to her briefly and hear how much she cared about my sister.

I prepared my speech with the goal of making everyone laugh at some of Rosanne's past antics and especially, to thank the two women who supported her through her illness. Her sons also spoke, one very briefly and one at length about how his mother was an angel and he adored her. I tried not to think back at all the times he had so brutally disrespected her over the years. He had been very mean to her at times, but after his mother died, he chose to focus on the good memories and forget the bad, which is healthy and normal I suppose. I have done the same with my father to a large extent. Forgiveness is the only way to move on with life.

Both of Rosanne's sons were very civil to me at the event and were proud to show off their three new babies and toddlers. Both their partners were very friendly, and I met some of their relatives who also came to pay their respects. It was a healing event for all of us to set aside our differences and share our love for Rosanne. I congratulated her son for pulling off a lovely tribute and gave both my nephews a large historical photo of their grandmother's extended family. I was very glad that I went.

# Her Estate

AFTER ROSANNE DIED, I WAS SHOCKED TO LEARN THAT SHE HAD NAMED me as her second executor, after her good friend Alison, who couldn't do the job because she had too many other obligations as the single parent of a young boy. I knew immediately that I would accept the role, since I had recently retired and knew enough about finances to do a good job. I felt it was the least I could do and that it would somehow bridge the huge gap between us, even though that was a ridiculous notion since she was already gone. I just felt it was the right thing to do and that her sons needed the best possible representation to get whatever amount of money was their due. They both had toddlers and desperately needed the cash. I knew it would be complicated because I would have to sell her house remotely and deal with her debts and several different job pensions, but I was determined. It was actually a pleasant surprise that she entrusted me to do the right thing and look after her boys' inheritance. It showed that she still held an underlying respect for me in spite of our estrangement and I was happy to oblige.

I knew things could get tense with her sons. Her younger son, who had been belligerent towards me and my husband for fifteen years, then approached me to ask if he could choose the lawyer, who was a friend of his. After a long pause, I said yes. This turned out to be a mistake, as the one person in the office I ended up dealing with was fairly incompetent. The whole thing got stuck in probate for a year and a half. I ended up selling the house twice, as the first deal fell through, and then renting it back to the owners so they could move in there faster. The only good thing to come out of this was that it mended fences between Rosanne's sons and I, and we miraculously remained civil the entire time. Mum was also pleased that I stepped up to handle her affairs. Everything worked out fine in the end. They each inherited a decent amount of money from her pensions and home sale, and it actually built a healthier bridge between us, for which I am grateful.

While going through her papers, it was shocking to read her medical report from the psychiatrist who handled her disability pension. Not only was she labeled as an alcoholic, but also the mood disorder, severe clinical depression and substance abuse were front and center. The sheer volume of prescription medications she was on was staggering. I wondered how any doctor could have loaded her up to this extent without fearing an overdose. Mum and I certainly did. It was no wonder she ended up at the psych ward in hospital for several months to wean her off these medications and set up a more reasonable protocol.

Reading this report made me feel upset and guilty for not making more of an effort to reconcile with Rosanne. Every time I saw her at Mum's over the preceding fifteen years, we would keep it light and avoid the real sticking points; the first being that she blamed me for abandoning her when she was struggling to raise her two young kids alone. She felt that I should have helped her more. The second was the deal we made when I bought her half of our parent's home. She regretted taking the deal as she saw property values rise in the years afterwards. She felt no gratitude towards me for taking care of Mum for ten years; she only felt jealousy of my time with Mum and bitterness that she was living far away. She could never accept that her own life choices could have played any part in these outcomes. She was always the victim.

All Rosanne's friends whom I have spoken to since her passing seem to have known that she was struggling mightily with mental health issues, even in her youth. They loved her because she was smart, funny, unique, and daring. It was never boring being with her, even if you were just sitting around talking. Everything became a joke, a poem, a doodle, or an exciting plan. If you were going to be her friend, you had to accept the highs with the lows, so some of her long-term friends were exceptionally devoted and caring people who I still admire to this day. I recognized the two wonderful women, Jenna and Alison, who were patient enough to stick by her through her cancer in my speech. To me, they were saints, and I will be forever grateful to them for trying to save her life. They stepped up when I couldn't. I was busy looking after our mother, but I still feel guilty at times. I'm glad she died with her sons at her bedside,

I couldn't bear the thought of her dying alone.

Now, as an adult, I find that I am drawn towards people who suffer from mental illness. I feel immediately comfortable with people who share similar disorders to my sister and father. I have three close friends who are bipolar and have been hospitalized. It's almost like I have a hidden secret radar for meeting them. I enjoy listening to them share their feelings and trying to help them. Perhaps this is why I was also drawn towards special education in my work as a teacher. I always found the neurotypical kids way too boring and wanted to work with those who struggled. I changed career paths halfway through my career to work with kids with various disabilities. I was much happier in this capacity and spent fifteen years helping families to build success for their children.

If there are any lessons to be learned from Rosanne's passing, I think it's that I may have had blinders on and never fully understood how severe her mental health issues were. When you are so close to someone, especially an older sibling who you look up to, it is easy to miss. As a kid, you revere them and believe they can do no wrong. You want to be like them, even if they make mistakes and fall down. You try to emulate the good parts of them and ignore the weaknesses.

It's only as an adult that you can start to be more objective and take stock of your own family dynamic. Your parents and siblings suddenly come into focus as human beings rather than gods. You can re-assess the relationships and ask other people who knew you well at that time for their different perspectives. In the end, there is no right or wrong, there are only memories and love.

# Estrangement and Regret

I HAVE MANY FRIENDS WHO HAVE LOST TOUCH WITH THEIR SIBLINGS over all kinds of family drama. Perceived favoritism in the wills and estates of parents often creates the kind of rift that we experienced, but often the damage is done much earlier than this. Differences in lifestyle are not uncommon. One sibling becomes very religious and tries to reform other family members. Drugs and alcohol are probably the most common culprits. I even know one man who left his wife and three kids to live as a recluse and never contacted them or his parents or siblings again for his remaining forty years. Sometimes there is just no good explanation.

It's now almost four years since Rosanne's death, which has been just enough time to reflect on what could have been done differently to sustain our relationship. There are a million scenarios where either one of us could have reached out with some gesture of kindness or forgiveness. I do wish I had gone to see her home on the Sunshine Coast, where she found her peace and independence from our family life. I definitely missed her raucous sense of humor for the twenty years of our estrangement. Nobody could surprise me or make me laugh in quite the same way. She had an absurdist outlook on the world that I really enjoyed. I loved witnessing the way she detected people's foibles so quickly and could see through any fake veneer. I'm sorry that she didn't get to know my daughter better. They would have shared a creative flair for the visual arts that I simply don't possess. I know that Rosanne would have loved to spend more time with her because she only had boys.

Am I guilt-ridden? Sometimes when I try to consider my sister more objectively as a mental health patient, I feel like I should have been more sympathetic. I imagine readers thinking of me as cold and cruel. The truth is, when you live with someone your whole life, you don't have this kind of standoffish clarity because everything they do impacts you in some way. Even if it's just indirectly, you know from childhood that any meltdown will sap the life out of your parents and their stress will be felt throughout the whole house. It becomes a part of your very being. Your family is a symbiotic clump of cells that can't exist independently; at least that's what you feel instinctively. When you finally become an adult and move out, you start to take control of your own life and realize that you can be happier and stronger on your own.

I think we both did the best we could under the circumstances. After leaving home, my priority became my relationship with my husband, caring for my own children and then my aged mother. I always worked full-time so my life was very busy, and Rosanne had moved several hours away. I'm grateful that we were still able to have a cup of tea together civilly at Mum's on occasion, otherwise I would have never seen her. I think that's better than a lot of siblings can say, even though her bitterness was always tangible under the surface. I think she really regretted being geographically so far away from Mum and resented me for stepping up to care for her. She was always jealous of the bond that Mum and I shared.

So, for you, dear reader, would I recommend adopting a more accommodating stance with your siblings as you get older? I think every family has its unique set of circumstances which define how we see the world. You may still be close to your siblings; this is laudable and also very lucky. I know so many who are estranged that it may even be the norm. Family feuds are rife. There is frequently one child who is the "black sheep" who everyone else has to support, both financially and emotionally.

Often, we are pressured by our parents to make amends because it hurts them to see us feuding. My own mother never gave up hope that Rosanne and I would reconcile, but she always put the onus on me to be the bigger person and fix the relationship. I don't think she felt like my sister was capable of changing anything, given her mental illness, and this was probably accurate. I just couldn't see a way to communicate with Rosanne without the rift over money coming into it. She always played the victim card and wanted me to fix her life. I just wasn't prepared to pay off all her debts to make her like me again.

I would encourage you to find your own happiness and if this includes one or more siblings, that's wonderful. Siblings are no different than friends, so try to treat them as such, if you can. Try to communicate using the same level of courtesy and respect you would with a friend. Just as you should let go of the friends who don't lift you up and make you feel good about yourself, the same goes for family members. Be unabashedly yourself and you will find your people. Life is too short to spend trying to fix broken relationships if the other party won't meet you halfway.

# A Better Life

As I reflect on my sister's passing, I can't help wondering how she might have had a happier life. Our parents' background influenced our upbringing due to the generational gap between what they had lived through and what Rosanne was experiencing in her young teens. The war generation had no notion of mental health care. During the sixties and seventies, the general public was fairly unaware of mental health diagnoses, such as anxiety, depression, or bipolar mood disorder. The term "nervous breakdown" was the blanket vernacular that covered anything out of the norm.

I still can't help but wonder why our mother never took Rosanne to see a therapist. I don't think the schools had any idea how to handle her and neither did my parents. They should have seen the writing on the wall and taken her disruptive behavior more seriously. Perhaps if she had seen a good psychiatrist, she could have avoided many of the pitfalls of her later life. Perhaps if they could have helped bolster her self-esteem, she could have chosen men who lifted her up instead of dragging her down.

Now that I have worked in the school system for thirty years, I am sure that in today's climate, a young teenager like Rosanne would have been referred for help. She would have at least gone to counseling for an extended period of time. There would have been discussions with our parents about getting professional help outside of the school system. Children are not permitted to stay at school when they are high as a kite, without even notifying the parents. This kind of negligence seems so unprofessional to me now, yet it really happened to my sister. How were all her red flags ignored? If she had been treated properly for bipolar depression at a young age, who knows how her life might have turned out differently? I can only speculate that her wild teens and twenties would have been somewhat tamer and less impulsive. She could have made more rational decisions, instead of running off with every macho idiot who gave her attention. Do I sound angry at the system? I think I am just disappointed.

I'm also angry at Rosanne for sabotaging our friendship with her outlandish, unbearable domestic situations. I'm disappointed that she never saw herself as good enough or worthy of a decent man who would love and respect her the way she deserved. I'm angry at her for being a lousy mother who couldn't cope and screaming at her toddlers to "Fuck off!" She allowed them to run wild and treat her disrespectfully to the point that it made me sick to my stomach to witness. I'm mad that she allowed her kids to grow, distribute and use drugs under her roof and under Grandma's roof, thereby putting our Mum in harm's way. I'm pissed that she would never listen or take any advice from me, Mum or anyone else who loved her out of sheer stubbornness. I'm mad at her for abusing her body so much that she got cancer and died too young unnecessarily. I've been told that this anger is a natural part of the grieving process.

Now I just feel sad and helpless when I think about her life. What a waste of potential. She was so smart, charming, and funny. She was beautiful and generous. Was she ever really happy? I have no idea, but I will choose to envision her driving her red Chevy Nova in the summer with the windows down, the stereo blasting, long hair blowing in the wind, and both of us singing "Here Comes My Girl" by Tom Petty at the top of our lungs. This is the sister I wish to remember.

# A Bipolar Life

SINCE ROSANNE HAS DIED, IT HAS OCCURRED TO ME THAT PERHAPS there was trauma in her childhood that I knew nothing about, which would explain her outlandish sexual behaviour, low self-esteem, and need for constant male attention and validation. I have racked my brain trying to imagine who, when, or where she could have been sexually abused, perhaps by an older boy or a man, but I have no idea. It would have had to have happened fairly young, because she was already very precocious around men when she was six, according to my gay uncle. He said it was uncomfortable to watch and be around. She was five years older than me, so I was not yet born when our family lived in Ontario. I do know that both parents were working soon after she was born, so perhaps there could have been some interaction with a babysitter that went terribly wrong. I will never know. I never asked Mum about this, but it would certainly explain a lot.

I recall reading her college psychology essay where she had done some self-reflection. She said she felt abandoned by our father in her early years because he was often away on business. A psychologist friend of mine said this perceived abandonment could definitely have been a real trauma for her. Mum also said that Dad didn't know how to be affectionate with children. After we spent the whole summer in England without Dad, he greeted his five-year-old Rosanne at the airport with a handshake. Mum thought this was very odd. Why was he withholding physical affection?

Then I considered intergenerational trauma. Dad had been forced to leave his parents behind when he was fifteen and lost them to the Nazis when he was seventeen. Could this trauma have been passed down to Rosanne? I am no expert, but I know that many psychologists believe this intergenerational trauma to be very real.2 There have been many psychological studies about Holocaust survivor's children and intergenerational trauma. Rosanne was very much like Dad in emotional make-up and personality, and he always said she was just like his grandmother. So perhaps she was destined to carry this psychological load from birth. Maybe it translated into the tremendous fear of abandonment by men which seemed to drive her needy behavior.

When she hit puberty, she definitely had periods of low mood and prolonged sadness where she would also sleep excessively and be very difficult to rouse. I remember trying to wake her up and it was so challenging. She had to drink a lot of very strong coffee and smoke a bunch of cigarettes to fully wake up.

Her severe depression since puberty made every menstrual cycle a nightmare. Every month through her teens, she would cry and wail like a caged animal to the point where I was really worried about her. Full moon was another time when she seemed to be adversely affected.

The treatment she received was for PMS back in the early seventies; taking Midol for cramps, which was basically caffeine and acetaminophen with an antihistamine. This helped her pain but did nothing for her mood. She would frequently leave school with this affliction, which didn't help her grades either. Depression often impairs focus, so learning was no doubt challenging and she got low marks except for in English and Drama, because she loved to write and perform.

She was treated with antidepressants beginning in her twenties and they generally worked well for her for some years but then they would lose their efficacy and she would switch to a new one. I know of at least three different brands she used over extended periods of years. Then, after her first child was born, in her late twenties, she experienced very severe postpartum depression for a whole year, despite medication.

Somewhere between the ages of thirty and forty, she told us that she had been diagnosed with a mood disorder and was given an additional set of medications for this. However, the word "bipolar" was never once mentioned. I never understood what "mood disorder" meant, other than she could fly off the handle into a nasty temper without warning, just like our father.

Our family doctor made this diagnosis on his own. I don't know why she was never referred to a psychiatrist at this point, but she definitely should have been. This wasn't his area of specialization, and she never got the kind of therapy she needed to change anything. Positive behavior support could have gone a long way towards helping Rosanne make changes in her life. It was already available in the 1980's when she was first seeking treatment.1

Now, looking back, I realize that all her wild high-risk behavior was probably the manic phase of a bipolar disorder. The way she would run off with strange men she had just met and disappear for a few days, taking drugs and having sex with them on a whim, indicated a complete loss of judgement. My family never understood this as part of a mood disorder; we just thought she was a "wild child". She put herself in some really dangerous situations, which created a darkness around her when she would not share with me. I think she knew when she had crossed a line into this danger zone, and she felt ashamed. How our parents ever slept at night is beyond me. They were so naive at times.

There's no doubt in my mind that her behavior around men was self-destructive. At the first meeting, she seemed like an intelligent, bold, strong woman. Then whenever she fell in love, she would regress into some pathetically doting, mothering state with her boyfriends, while never expecting anything in return other than sex. It was a bizarre transformation to behold. I felt like shaking her and yelling at her to wake up and see these men for what they were: freeloaders; users; giant babies with no redeemable qualities or interests to speak of. None of them were a match for her intelligence or wit and they all bored me to tears. There must have been such a base-level sexual drive between them that just got a hold of her and held her spellbound. It certainly defied logic.

She also didn't have the decision-making skills to make long term decisions, follow through on a plan, or manage money. This is also typical behavior for bi-polar patients. She would invariably spend all her money on Christmas presents for her kids and come running to Mum for help with rent in January. She was always overly generous with her friends and lived paycheque to paycheque her whole life. Thank goodness she qualified for a disability pension eight years before she died because otherwise, she would have been struggling financially when she got sick with cancer. It's a good thing she stopped working when she did because she needed to start treatment and get a mastectomy shortly after this.

She also self-medicated with cigarettes and marijuana her whole life and was a recreational drinker. I remember her favorite drink, other than beer, when we were hanging out together in her twenties was bourbon and soda. She was never an alcoholic and I think she could have quite easily given it up altogether. The same cannot be said for nicotine or THC. She tried to quit smoking several times using "the patch" but it never took. To my knowledge, she never gave up smoking pot, even after her lung cancer diagnosis. She admitted to me that she was addicted to it. I know there has been much debate over whether marijuana is a behavioral or chemical addiction, but whatever the case, she used it daily.

I also considered how Rosanne's apparent addiction to smoking pot might have affected her mental health, so I began looking online for studies on how cannabis affects bipolar patients. "While some more recent studies have found benefits of using CBD (cannabinoids) to treat bipolar, "there have been numerous studies on the link between bipolar disorder and cannabis. These studies feature in a 2017 review from the Alcohol and Drug Abuse Institute (ADAI).

The report found a link between cannabis use and the following health issues:

-developing bipolar at an earlier age

-longer or worse manic episodes

-higher likelihood of suicide attempts

-rapid cycling or quickly shifting from manic to depressive episodes

-suicide ideation in people who were heavy users of THC"[4]

The report also highlighted a 2015 study by Trusted Source, which found that people with bipolar disorder who used cannabis were less likely to go into remission for their condition than those who did not."[5]

"In addition, an older study from 2011, Trusted Source found that people with bipolar disorder who engaged in problematic cannabis use had higher levels of disability and more manic, depressive, and psychotic symptoms."[6]

In summation, "the ADAI report concluded there was more evidence of negative effects of cannabis on bipolar disorder than positive ones."[7]

In spite of this research, I feel that if her cannabis use brought her some pain or stress relief during her cancer, so much the better.

Rosanne finally saw a psychiatrist in her fifties, when she could no longer work and was required to do this as part of her disability pension claim. This was the first time in her life that anyone tried to get her pill popping under control. However, it was too little too late because she developed breast cancer shortly thereafter and her health gradually began to fail. I always wonder how her life might have been different if she had sought professional help sooner. It seemed like many years were wasted stubbornly pretending she could take care of herself instead of accessing the supports that were available.

When she got breast cancer and then lung cancer, she refused chemotherapy and radiation for reasons I will never know. Possibly, she didn't want to travel by ferry into Vancouver for these treatments. Instead, she opted for a new drug trial. I'm not sure how these drugs interacted with her other prescriptions, but it was clear that for the last five years of her life she was taking an unsafe quantity of pain pills.

She also had a tendency to abuse "downers", such as Ativan, which has a strong calming effect. She would take them whenever she had an appointment with her oncologist and, in retrospect, she should not have been driving. For a while she somehow got a hold of some Percocet, which contains an opioid. This may have been the drug she had to be weaned off in the psych ward. I'm not sure. I only remember her telling me how wonderful it was.

I'm not sure that her family doctor in her fifties did her any favors either. Her friend Jenna, who often took her to appointments, said that her GP was all too willing to prescribe Rosanne anything she wanted. As a psych nurse, Rosanne was perfectly aware of what was available. I suppose desperate times called for desperate measures, but this sounded like a vicious cycle to me; one that required two months in the psych ward "getting clean" of this toxic cocktail.

Being in chronic pain is the worst possible affliction and I honestly try not to think about how hard it must have been towards the end of her life. In a way, I was lucky I did not have to witness her passing. Or I was simply too much of a coward to face another barrage of hatred from Neil in order to attend at her bedside. Her sons were with her at the end, and it must have been a terrible time. I can only hope the nurses gave her enough morphine to make her comfortable.

So generally, I would say that it is disappointing that Rosanne largely missed the boat on proper treatment. I could also partially blame our parents' generation for a general lack of understanding of psychological problems and what kind of help was available, but what would be the point? Nowadays, my friends with bipolar disorder have much wider treatment options, including ECT (electroconvulsive therapy), (rTMS) repetitive transcranial magnetic stimulation, CBT (cognitive behavior therapy), and a wide variety of pharmacological innovations.3 So, hopefully outcomes are better these days when a patient seeks help.

My sister lived her final years away from the crowded city and far enough away from us, her prying family, who always held unrealistic expectations for her. She lived in a small, quiet seaside town across the water by ferry. She continued to walk on the beach every day with her beloved old dog until she was hospitalized in her final days. I truly hope she found solace contemplating the ocean, as I do now. I think we were both drawn back to our childhood days in Tofino, which were some of the happiest times of our lives.

# Footnotes

1) Overview and History of Positive Behavior Support
   **Author:** Glen Dunlap, Wayne Sailor, Robert H. Horner et al
   **Publication:** Springer eBook
   **Publisher:** Springer Nature
   **Date:** Jan 1, 2009
   © *2009, Springer Science Business Media B.V*
   https://link.springer.com/chapter/10.1007/978-0-387-09632-2_1

2) Donieli, Y. (1985). The treatment and prevention of long-term effects and intergenerational transmission of victimization: A lesson from Holocaust survivors and their children.
   © C. R. Figley (Ed.), *Trauma and its wake* (pp. 295-313). New York: Brunner/Mazel.
   https://scholar.google.ca/scholar?q=intergenerational+trauma+Holocaust+survivors+children&hl=en&as_sdt=0&as_vis=1&oi=scholart

3) Cognitive dysfunction in major depression and bipolar disorder: Assessment and treatment options
   ©Glenda M. MacQueen MD, PhD, FRCPC, Katherine A. Memedovich, BHSc (candidate)

*Footnotes*

First published: 29 September 201
https://onlinelibrary.wiley.com/doi/full/10.1111/pcn.12463
©1999-2022 John Wiley & Sons, Inc.

**4)** Effects of Marijuana on Mental Health: Bipolar Disorder
Considering Locked vs. Unlocked Treatment Facilities
Susan A. Stoner, PhD, Research Consultant
University of Washington ©2017 for ADAI (Alcohol and Drug Abuse Administration)

**5)** Impact of Cannabis Use on Long-Term Remission in Bipolar I and Schizoaffective Disorder
Sung-Wan Kim,1 Seetal Dodd,2,3 Lesley Berk,2,3,4 JaYahshri Kulkarni,5 Anthony de Castella,5 Paul B. Fitzgerald,5 Jae-Min Kim,1 Jin-Sang Yoon,1 and Michael Berk 2,3,6,7
Author information Article notes Copyright and License information© 2015 Korean Neuropsychiatric Association

**6)** Cannabis involvement in individuals with bipolar disorder
Arpana Agrawal 1, John I Nurnberger Jr, Michael T Lynskey, Bipolar Genome Study

**Collaborators**
• **Bipolar Genome Study**: John R Kelsoe, Tiffany Greenwood, Caroline M Nievergelt, Thomas B Barrett, Rebecca McKinney, Paul D Shilling, Nicholas Schork, Erin N Smith, John Nurnberger, Howard J Edenberg, Chun-Yu Liu, Judith A Badner, William Scheftner, William B Lawson, Evaristus A Nwulia, Maria Hipolito, John Rice, William Byerley, Francis McMahon, Thomas G Schulze, Wade Berrettini, James B Potash, Peter P Zandi, Pamela B Mahon, Melvin McInnis, Dominic Craig, Szabolcs Szelinger

# Affiliation

●1

●Dept. of Psychiatry, Washington University School of Medicine, Saint Louis, MO 63110, USA. arpana@wustl.edu
●Psychiatry Res
● . 2011 Feb 28;185(3):459-61. doi: 10.1016/j.psychres.2010.07.007. Epub 2010 Jul 31.

7)What to know about cannabis and bipolar disorder https://www.medicalnewstoday.com/articles/315187#the-bottom-line
© 2004-2022 Healthline Media UK Ltd, Brighton, UK,

# Bibliography

1) https://www.sheknows.com/health-and-wellness/articles/1995052/newborn-baby-mini-period/
SheKnows is a part of Penske Media Corp. ©2022 SheMedia LLC. All rights reserved.

2) 10faq.com/health/common-mood-disorders/2/
© 2022 10FAQ All Rights Reserved.
Atomiq Technologies Inc.

3) facty.com/ailments/stress/10-symptoms-of-mood-disorder
© 2022 Assemblies Technology Inc.

4) An Unquiet Mind: A Memoir of Moods and Sadness © 1996 by Kay Redfield Jamison; First Vintage Books Edition

5) What Are Bipolar Disorders? www.psychiatry.org ©2022 American Psychiatric Association
Reviewed Jan 2021 by Molly Howland MD and Alex El Sehamy MD, APA/APAF Fellow

# Also by Naomi Lane

Her first book, a humorous memoir, is called The Ultimate Cat: A Baby-Boomer's Guide to Retirement.

Her second book, a novel: The Ordinary Life of Nadia Lewis, tells of a lifelong friendship between two women.

Her third book, a novel: On Golden Land, tells of seven friends who move to New Mexico to live communally and grow marijuana.

She also has a weekly blog called The Friday Blog, which you can follow at: naomiplane.com

You can find her on Twitter and Instagram @namaferd

On Facebook @ The Friday Blog by Naomi P Lane

Manufactured by Amazon.ca
Bolton, ON